HEALING
through
PRAYER

THE POWER WITHIN
Healing Through Prayer

A one-hour video documentary presenting memorable highlights from the interviews featured in this book.

Accompanied by a study manual, this video is an excellent resource for the church or the home.

ISBN 1-55126-234-7

HEALING
through
PRAYER

Health Practitioners Tell the Story

Larry Dossey, Herbert Benson,
John Polkinghorne, and Others

with a foreword by Peter Downie

Anglican Book Centre
Toronto, Canada

1999
Anglican Book Centre
600 Jarvis Street
Toronto, Ontario
M4Y 2J6

Copyright © Anglican Book Centre

Cover photo: Gary S. and Vivian Chapman/The Image Bank, 1999.

Canadian Cataloguing in Publication Data

Dossey, Larry, 1940-
    Healing through prayer: health practitioners tell the story

ISBN 1-55126-229-0

1. Spiritual healing. 2. Prayer. I. Benson, Herbert, 1935- .
II. Polkinghorne, J.C., 1930-   . III. Title.

BL65.M4D67 1999   291.3'1   C99-931207-3

CONTENTS

FOREWORD

PETER DOWNIE, *the author of best-selling books on healing and Canadian broadcasting, is a well-known television and radio host.*

You probably didn't find this book in the mystery section of your local library or bookstore, but don't be fooled. This book is full of mystery stories — good ones — although not in the traditional "who-done-it" genre. If the people you'll meet in these pages debated the question, "Who done it?" they might eventually arrive at a consensus — and I'd love to hear the debate. But the main point is that reading their stories will leave you with a sense of wonder and also hope.

This engaging mystery is about healing through the power of prayer. Neither P. D. James nor Patricia Cornwell could phrase it better than Barbara Shoomski, a Cree spiritual caregiver at the Health Sciences Centre in Winnipeg, when she says, "I was standing beside her bed and I was just praying from the depths of my being, and all of a sudden I had this feeling come through me and into her. And I knew that God was there. I knew. I could feel it. It drained my body."

In addition to the first-hand accounts of medical recoveries, there are wonderfully provocative ideas in this book. More and more of us, interested in living and being well, are embracing something truly remarkable, easier to identify than to explain: the power of prayer to heal. As a result, our whole concept of health care is expanding. This revolution is driven by two understandings. The first is that, to be genuinely healthy, we must take into account mind and spirit as well as body. The second is that the priority given by Western medicine to *curing* rather than *healing* has gone about as far as it can.

In some respects, Western medicine has become a victim of its own success. The truly miraculous technological advances of the late twentieth century present us with extraordinarily difficult ethical and moral questions. Questions like "What is the quality of a life extended by medical means?" and "Given limited financial resources, whose life is more worthy to receive a particular treatment?"

It is time for a shift in thinking on the part of those who, as Harvard's Dr. Herbert Benson says in the following pages, "expect health care to be done to us, not by us." "What's important," suggests this medical pioneer, "is not what the doctor believes in, but what the patient believes in."

Curing implies that painful symptoms will be relieved or disappear through the efforts of someone else, most likely a professional medical practitioner. *Healing* implies controlling suffering at every level. And it can blossom only from within.

We live in a fast, noisy, competitive culture where the idea of winning has become supreme. It's not surprising that this poison has leached into the thinking of health care professionals and consumers alike. Death is viewed as the great opponent to be stared down, conquered, and overcome. The emotional and philosophical distortions arising from this kind of thinking make it even tougher to understand that real healing requires us to live in harmony and balance within ourselves and with our surroundings. If disease is about broken bodies and spirits, healing is concerned with wholeness.

It seems to me that, only when we connect with our inner silence and profit from its richness, can we heal. The door to that inner silence can be opened through the use of prayer and meditation. In that silence, we recognize a blessed sense of grace that flows from a greater force. In that silence, even as the extreme moment of dying approaches, we recognize the difficult truth that death is a natural and necessary act. Healing can mean a sense of acceptance, of completion, and of serenity.

The eminent physicist and Anglican priest John Polkinghorne believes prayer works, not "because there are more fists beating on the heavenly door to attract the divine attention, but because more wills are aligned with the divine will to bring about good consequences in the unfolding history of the world."

Every healer eventually mentions the need to be filled with good intentions and to keep an open heart and mind towards others. For example, Joan Halifax, a Buddhist teacher in New Mexico, believes that, "to be able to make whole, we need a deep and open heart from which prayer naturally arises."

Larry Dossey, author of several books on prayer and healing, says, "If we want to be good physicians, we simply can't run away from the power of love."

As true as this may be, in reality most doctors don't have time for lunch, let alone for empathy. And even if they want to bring personal concern into their practice, the treadmill of the Western medical system prevents them from pursuing their inclination. Surely that's part of the reason why bookstores display rows and rows of books on health and healing — and, where I shop, even a section devoted to death and dying. All of us are getting smarter about the rich and complex relationship between body and mind. As we consider that "the greater force" isn't *out there* somewhere, but is *within* each of us, we understand that to be healthy means to be a partner with the greater force and to reclaim a measure of control.

One of the great misconceptions of the twentieth century is that science and religion are mutually exclusive. As that idea withers on the vine of experience, the new growth that is being revealed is filled with unlimited possibilities. "We have a power to understand that goes very far beyond anything that arises from the necessity to survive," says John Polkinghorne. "The paradigms of science are shifting. Quantum theory, chaos theory, and other extremely interesting ... advances in science have shown us that the world is more subtle and more supple than that. Science now speaks of probabilities and patterns, not predictable certainties."

The choice between the rational world of science and the more intuitive sphere of prayer and belief is a false option. As Larry Dossey points out, "Choosing one over the other makes a schizophrenic division in our lives." Healing is about erasing divisions like these.

And it is about erasing divisions between ourselves and the world around us, and between ourselves and the greater force. In the following pages you'll meet Rabbi Ronald Weiss, who suggests that a union with one's community, fostered and nurtured through prayer, is critical. "It's not so much the answer that matters, but the feeling that God is listening that is of critical importance.... Feeling that God cares about you can give you tremendous spiritual strength, and with spiritual strength you can overcome virtually any physical circumstance."

If you're sceptical, you're not alone.

Read the words of Teresa Ardanaz, a Toronto mother of two, diagnosed with cancer. Her healing journey included prayers offered over the telephone. "Two years ago," she begins, "I might have found it laughable to think that there could be a connection [between healing and prayer], but when it happened, it was very real and very moving. But the strength to live isn't just the result of wanting another year of life. It results from loving people."

We must bring a questioning, sceptical mind to all of this, if only because the ideas of healing and faith have been so exploited. Both are gold-mines of opportunity for the unscrupulous to take advantage of people who are struggling through the most dire and frightening of life circumstances. But aided by the careful research such as that presented in this book, and by alert senses, the soft whisper of an inner voice will lead us to understand what's real and what's not.

In the end, healing through prayer remains a great mystery, but this much is crystal clear and deceptively simple: it is all about caring and loving. There's no easy way to understand why children die of cancer, or why loved ones are taken from us, sometimes heartbreakingly early. These are profoundly deep wounds in search of healing, and in that pain it may be hard to accept the judgement of C. S. Lewis that "the hardness of God is kinder than the softness of men."

Wendy Dimmock, who has worked as a nurse in Africa, Britain, and now in Canada, says that she remembers a doctor telling her that "Christian healing is the strength to live, the strength to suffer, and the strength to die." Her words echo St. Augustine's counsel that we should treat our bodies as if we would live forever and our souls as if we would die tomorrow.

Part 1

SCIENCE
AND
SPIRITUALITY

SCIENCE AND RELIGION ARE COMPLEMENTARY

JOHN POLKINGHORNE *is the author of many books on the interaction between science and religion. After twenty-five years as a theoretical physicist, he left his career to train for the priesthood in the Anglican Church, and returned to Cambridge University in England, where he was president of Queens' College until 1998.*

How do you reconcile your life as a scientist with your life as a priest?

I can't remember when I wasn't part of the worshipping and believing community. I enjoyed being a scientist, but after about twenty-five years, I felt I had done my bit for theoretical physics, and the time had come to do something else. Because religion was important to me, it seemed worthwhile to seek ordination. I see God's guiding hand in the decision, but it came about through circumstances, reflection, the advice of friends, and talking to my wife, rather than through any dramatic experience such as hearing a heavenly voice on the road to Damascus.

I have never felt any conflict or lack of balance between the scientific and religious sides of my life. Of course, there have been puzzles about how each relates to the other, but I never felt I had to choose between them. I need the insights of science, and I need the insights of religion.

What is seen as the opposition between science and religion requires a historical rather than a logical explanation. There have been moments when science and religion have obviously had difficulties with each other. The famous stories of Galileo and of Darwin are examples, although both of these are much more complicated episodes than the popular caricatures suggest. But logically there isn't a contradiction between science and religion because they are both trying to find the truth through motivated belief. They are, of course, looking at different aspects of the truth. Science is looking at an impersonal world that it can put to the test. Religion is looking at a personal and a transpersonal world involving God, where testing has to give way to trusting. But they have enough in common, I think, to be friends rather than enemies.

Do you think that science and spirituality are coming together again?

We are living in a time when there is a coming together of science and religion, partly because people realize that, although science is very powerful and very effective, it has an extremely limited view of the world. We can see this clearly in matters of health and healing. If you're going to deal with people not as biochemical machines but as whole persons, then you have to consider aspects of people about which science has little to say but of which tradition offers a great deal of understanding. We know, for example, that when we are treating a disease, we must take into account the sick person's attitude, expectations, and powers of hope. In this simple example there is a coming together of science and religion to develop an embracing account of what it means to be a person — and also to describe the nature of reality.

We are not simply spiritual beings who happen to be housed in physical bodies. We are beings who have both spiritual and mental, as well as physical, aspects. If we are to be healthy, all these aspects of our persons must be integrated in our lives, and the treatment we receive to assist our recovery from troubles, including sickness, must recognize them all.

In the scientific world during the last thirty or forty years, particularly in the physical sciences, we have come to realize that questions arise from science which are not in themselves scientific in character. They go beyond science, so to speak. One is: why is science possible at all? What makes it possible for us to understand the physical world as perfectly and profoundly as we do? Of course, at the level of everyday experience, we have to understand the world in order to survive. If we didn't know that it was a bad idea to walk off the top of a high cliff, we wouldn't be around for very long. But Newton could see that the force of gravity that makes the cliff dangerous is also what holds the solar system together. Later on, Einstein could expand this in a generalization that describes the whole universe in which we live. We have a power to understand that goes very far beyond anything that arises from the necessity to survive.

To return, then, to the question: *why* is science possible? In other words, *why* is the world intelligible? Science provides no answer; it just gets on with the job. I think that science is possible because we live in a world that is a creation. That is why it is orderly. Since we are creatures made in the image of our creator, our minds are able to discern the beautiful patterns of nature that science investigates and describes.

But some events that may be part of the pattern are not beautiful. How do we explain natural disasters and also the evil and violence for which humans themselves are responsible? The greatest problem for religious believers is undoubtedly the problem of evil and suffering. In science we see a world that is very beautiful and orderly, but when we look at human history we see a world in which there is a great deal of suffering. It includes a great many things that seem contrary to the will of a God, assuming that there is a God behind what is happening in the world. The problem of evil and suffering is extremely important and extremely perplexing. I think it holds more people back from religious belief than anything else. Even those of us who are religious believers are always conscious of the difficulties it raises.

I think the answer lies in recognizing that, in bringing the world into existence, God allowed the other truly to be itself. Creatures are not puppets in a theatre where God pulls every string and makes everything happen. We are allowed to be ourselves, just as the world is allowed to make itself. That is the theological understanding of evolution.

Somebody once asked: what was God's will in the Lisbon earthquake? It occurred on All Saints' Day, 1755. The churches were full, and when they collapsed, 50,000 people were killed. It was a terrible natural disaster. The answer is very hard, but I think true: God's will was that the elements of the earth's crust should behave in accordance with their nature. God allows tectonic plates to be themselves, and that means they will slip and cause earthquakes. The world is allowed to be itself. I believe that God wills neither the act of a murderer nor the incidence of a cancer, but allows both to happen in a creation to which God has given freedom.

Does God ever intervene in the course of nature?

The scientific discoveries of the twentieth century have helped us to understand that the world is flexible and open in relation to the future. Eighteenth- and nineteenth-century science conceived of the world as a gigantic piece of clockwork, operating in a rigidly mechanical way. We know now that this isn't true. The paradigms of science are shifting. Quantum theory, chaos theory, and other extremely interesting and important advances in science have shown us that the world is more subtle and more supple than that. Science now speaks of probabilities and patterns, not predictable certainties.

Conventional physics has used the concept of energy to explain that things work by pushing and pulling. But as we study more complex systems, in which we see very beautiful patterns of ordered developments, we realize that we must consider not only energy in explaining what is going on, but also what one might call *information*. By information, I mean the process of pattern formation. I think that God interacts with the world in the forming of patterns; that is, in the shaping of events. And it is by these patterns that we bring about our willed actions.

For example, how does my intention to raise my arm bring about the actual raising of it? Of course, as a result of my intention, energy is transmitted to the muscles. Yet raising my arm is an action of the "whole me." I *decide* to raise my arm. I can tell the difference between raising my arm and somebody stimulating it to make it jump up. In some very complex and generalized sense, our actions in and interactions with the world are like my deciding to raise my arm. They depend on the formation of patterns of thought and movement.

We have all experienced significant coincidences. Each event by itself is perfectly understandable, but the way in which they come together makes significance. It is an example of what is happening in the world being the result not only of the flow of energy, but also of the pattern-forming effects of information. Since pattern formation involves clusters of events, we should take significant coincidences seriously. It may be possible to understand some of the miracles in the gospels this way. When Jesus calmed the storm, that squall over the Lake of Galilee may have been coming to a perfectly natural end, but it ended at the significant moment when Jesus was awakened and said, "Peace, be still."

But then there are radical miracles so unnatural that you cannot imagine how they have happened except by God's direct action. The resurrection of Jesus is the most striking and most important example. We have to understand these events as being rooted deeper in reality than we can otherwise probe. They are windows that open onto the way God acts in the world: not by intervention but by interacting with an ordered universe which also has the freedom to be itself. Christians do not believe that God is a celestial conjurer who plays tricks to astonish people. We believe that there must be consistency in what God does.

To suggest that God intervenes is to suggest that God does things not consistently but occasionally, as if he watches what's going on and then suddenly decides to change this or that, or to help this or that person. But God's consistency in interacting with the world does not override the world. Nor is it dreary uniformity. In new, unprecedented circumstances, God can do unprecedented things. Miracles always involve the particular circumstances of the occasion. In relation to Jesus, who, we believe, uniquely presents God in human life, the circumstances are particular indeed!

I believe that in this open-ended world, we play some part in bringing about the future. God plays some part in bringing about the future, and God acts in the world, but God allows us to act as well.

Is prayer one of the means by which we play a part in bringing about the future, including praying for the healing of sick people?

I believe that we have power to act in the world and that God also has retained power to act in the world. In prayer we're seeking to align those two actions as closely as possible. We offer in prayer our power to bring about a little bit of the future, to be taken by God and used by God to bring about his good and perfect world for the future. I like to use the illustration of laser light. Laser light is powerful because it is what physicists call *coherent*. That is to say, it is made up of waves, but the waves are all in step. All the crests come together and add up; all the troughs come together and add down. In light whose waves are out of step, crests and troughs cancel each other out. In prayer we are seeking a laser-like coherence between human will and divine will, and when those two wills are aligned, I believe things can happen that would not happen if they were at cross-purposes.

If we're always fighting against God, either consciously or unconsciously, then we will frustrate some of God's good purposes. But if we are open and prepared to offer ourselves and collaborate with God, that attitude will have consequences not only for us but also for other people, because everything is linked together in the world. Knowing that everything is linked together helps to explain why the praying of a lot of people for the same thing can achieve remarkable effects. These effects come about not because there are more fists beating on the heavenly door to attract the divine attention, but because more wills are aligned with the divine will to bring about good consequences in the unfolding history of the world.

In the gospels, Jesus encourages us to ask for things with very embarrassing directness. But when he said, "Ask and you will receive," I don't think he meant that God is a sort of heavenly Father Christmas who gives you a blank cheque to fill in as you like. "I'd like to be a billionaire tomorrow, God, please." But I do think that Jesus calls us to say what we truly want. When we pray, we express what we really value and what we really want to see happening. In the gospel a blind man comes to Jesus and Jesus asks, "What do you want?" What he wants is perfectly obvious: he's blind and he wants his sight! But he has to say so — to commit himself — before he's healed. I think God takes our values and wishes seriously. God, of course, also has to take seriously what other people value and want to happen. The vicar wants a fine day on Saturday for the church fête; the farmer wants rain for his crops. God has to work out the balance.

Nobody can talk about prayer without acknowledging the mystery of individual human destiny. When you pray earnestly

for someone who is very seriously ill, you are praying for healing; that is, for wholeness. That wholeness might come through
physical recovery, and that is probably what most people hope
will happen. Or it might come from accepting the destiny of
imminent death. I've witnessed very moving circumstances in
which the end of people's lives has been transformed by their
being able to accept the coming of death. They have a positive
death. However, there are obvious disappointments: the sick
persons or those praying for them may have deeply wished for
a recovery, which fails to come. Every person and every person's situation is different. There is no single outcome which
everybody can expect to unfold. There is a destiny for you, a
destiny for me.

There is disagreement over whether prayer for healing can
work only when the person prayed for is aware of the prayers
or only when those who are praying are close by. Since I think
of prayer as being very much a personal contact between an
individual and God, it is difficult for me to imagine prayer having some effect on people who do not know they are being
prayed for. I would need to examine the evidence very care-
fully before I could accept that prayer works that way. Even
then, I would feel that prayer is likely to be more effective where
there is collaboration between the person being prayed for and
those who are praying — and of course with God also. The
more personal and explicit the situation, the greater will be the
power of prayer to bring healing.

Some years ago, I suddenly fell very ill for the first time in
my life, and I had an emergency operation. I was lying there
with drips keeping me alive, my whole life narrowed to the
limits of the hospital bed. God seemed very far-away, and
prayer seemed almost impossible. But I was very conscious of
being prayed for. I knew my family and my church and some
Anglican nuns who are friends of mine were praying for me. I

was sustained by the prayers of others at a time when I couldn't pray myself. Although I might have been sustained also by the prayers of people I didn't know were praying for me, I think that the knowing was in itself helpful. It was as if those who were praying had said, "Don't worry. If you can't reach out to God yourself in your weakness, we'll be carriers, so to speak, of the communication between God and you." I learned something of what it means to speak of the communion of saints: that there is a collective experience of prayer, and prayer, though it is individual, also involves the company of the faithful.

Can prayer be used as a means of harming someone else?

The psalms are very interesting as prayers because they are extremely frank. In the psalms, people thank God with great joy. But they also protest to God in very frank and straightforward terms, and they curse their enemies. Some psalms contain curses so terrible that those psalms are often omitted in Christian worship. I don't think they should be omitted, because the cursing psalms represent feelings in the human heart, gut feelings that should not be indulged, but which we must acknowledge before God, so that God can cleanse us of them.

There are people who curse in earnest, and there are evil forces at work in the world. It would be very foolish to dismiss the possibility that there are evil spiritual forces that can be contacted and collaborated with. The most obvious example is the Holocaust. It can partly be explained by noting that there were determined and evil men leading the Nazis; that there was a political system that inculcated unhesitating obedience to the state; that people were scared for their lives and looked the other way when the cattle trucks rattled through the village.

But when you've taken all these things into account, the weight of evil involved seems to exceed what can be explained in human terms. No doubt, in a sort of reversal of prayer, some people try to invoke evil forces and collaborate with them.

It's a mystery why these evil forces should be allowed to have some sort of will with which people can align themselves, just as they can align themselves with God's will. Although some satanic practices are foolish mumbo-jumbo, there may be real satanic practices in which people give themselves to serve an evil cause. I think such people in the end destroy themselves spiritually.

Nothing perplexes the writers of the Old Testament more than the prosperity of the wicked. We tend to worry about why bad things happen to good people; they worried more about why good things happen to bad people.

There is no simple answer to either question, partly because the world contains accidents. Things just happen because they are allowed to happen in a creation that is not God's puppet theatre. For example, the same biochemical processes that have enabled cells to mutate and produce new forms of life — in other words, the very process that drives evolution and is responsible for the complexity of life — also allow other cells to mutate and become malignant. Science helps theology here by showing that the presence of cancer in the world is not due to the creator's callousness or incompetence; it is a necessary cost of a world allowed to make itself and to evolve richer and richer forms of life. In such a world, events like those malignancies just happen. They are not God's punishment; they are part of the pattern. A world that is allowed to be itself will inevitably contain blind alleys as well as fruitful paths.

Knowing all this does not remove the perplexity and the anguish we feel when bad things happen to good people, or the indignation we feel when good things happen to bad people.

But this world does not provide an automatic reward for either good or evil. However, I think that in a life beyond this world people will see themselves as they really are. That will be a painful realization for all of us — truly a form of judgement. Then we will, I think, be offered the opportunity to be purged of the evil we have done. Some may accept and some may not accept.

What is the future of the dialogue between science and religion?

I hope that, in the next fifty years, we'll see very positive interaction between science and religion. Each has important things to say to the other. During the last thirty or forty years the physical sciences have become acutely aware of the order and beauty and fruitfulness of the world, and some suggest that behind it lies a divine mind and purpose.

I think we are gradually realizing the poverty of a merely specialist view — a merely physical or merely biological picture, for example — and I hope we move in the direction of a more integrated account of human beings. In particular, scientists need to concentrate more on the human sciences, such as psychology, in order to understand what it means to be a person. But that's an area in which religion has extremely important insights and interests.

From the investigations of depth psychology, we have learned that we are much more than we are conscious of being. We have a rational ego — the part of us that articulates things — of which we are aware all the time. But scientists have been learning that there are more profound depths to human nature than we are usually aware of. Religion has always known this. St. Augustine, one of the great early Christian thinkers, was a man of tremendous introspective insight and anticipated many of the twentieth-century discoveries of depth psychology. Religion has always seen people as being more than their bodies, more even than their minds. It recognizes a spiritual dimension, the area in which our contact with God is most profound and effective. I hope that through the dialogue between science and religion we shall all be encouraged to recognize the spiritual dimension and to learn more about it. The specialization of the modern world tends to compartmentalize us. But these deeper aspects can be seen only if we look at the totality of things.

SCIENTIFIC RESEARCH CONFIRMS THE VALUE OF PRAYER IN HEALING

LARRY DOSSEY, *M.D.*, *a best-selling author and medical doctor in Santa Fe, New Mexico, is Co-chairman of the Panel on Mind/Body Interventions, National Institute of Health.*

~∾~

As a scientifically trained physician, how did you become involved in investigating the value of prayer in healing?

My first exposure to prayer was while growing up in a fundamentalist Christian environment in Texas. When I went away to medical school and encountered the titanic conflict between science and religious faith, I became a thorough-going agnostic. So when I became a physician, I was convinced that prayer, although it might make people feel better, certainly had no place in my treatment of sick people.

Early in my practice, I had some experiences with patients who had fatal illnesses. These people did not get adequate treatment, yet they were prayed for and they recovered completely. I was stunned by these experiences, but it was not until many years later that I began to take all of this seriously. At that time, I stumbled blindly on a body of evidence that I found utterly compelling — scientific studies evaluating the impact of distant intercessory prayer. Like most physicians, I didn't know this body of information even existed. It must be counted as one of the best-kept secrets in modern medical science. Many of these studies are utterly precise, but they were too controversial to have been taken into modern medicine and medical education. Fortunately, that is now changing.

After immersing myself in that body of knowledge for many years, I wrote three books about it, and this changed my life. It modified tremendously the way I treated patients. I got to the point of believing that withholding prayer from my patients might be like withholding a needed medication or surgical procedure. These studies definitely showed that prayer could have a positive healing effect on patients and might even be able to save their lives.

The studies — about 150 of them — have been done in reputable institutions, such as medical schools and universities. Most of them are what we call randomized controlled double-blind studies. This means that neither the individual receiving the prayer nor the physicians or nurses or health care team are aware of who is receiving prayer and who isn't. The prayed-for group is compared to the group who do not receive the prayer.

If you can show that prayer works for non-humans who don't think positively, such as rats, mice, bacteria, yeast, and various sorts of cells, then you can refute the sceptics' allegations that improvement in patients' health is merely the effect of expectation, or the placebo response. Together, the non-human studies and the human studies are a powerful set of data showing, in my judgement, that however one wishes to explain these effects, prayer is a powerful factor in healing.

How does prayer work?

People have searched for explanations about how it might work. Some have suggested that if you have an empathic, loving, prayerful thought for me, you could be transferring some sort of subtle energy to me. The problem with this explanation is that, although researchers have diligently explored whether or not any sort of subtle energy is transferred between the two people, no one has ever been able to discover any. If some sort of energy were being transferred between the person praying and the recipient of the prayer, you would expect the prayer to be more powerful at close distances than from afar. But the studies show that the effectiveness of the prayer is not altered by distance.

Also, if some sort of energy were being transferred, you should be able to block it by putting the recipient of the prayer in a lead- or metal-lined container called a Faraday cage. You can do this in experiments with animals or plants or bacteria. Actually, in a few of these experiments, a human being has been put in one of these containers. But the researchers discovered that the effect is equal inside the container or outside it. In other words, you cannot block, or shield, the effect of the prayer.

This would not be the case if some sort of energy were involved. So if energy is being transferred from mind to mind, we can't find any scientific evidence of it.

Dr. Herbert Benson of Harvard University believes that the effects of prayer can be explained by noting that it causes a relaxation response, and the relaxation promotes healing. For over twenty years, he has beautifully explored the effects of prayer and meditation on the individual who is engaged in it, and he has found that there is a uniform physiological response to prayer. For example, the body seems to enjoy the experience of praying or meditating. The metabolism quiets, the heart rate slows down, the blood pressure falls. Other researchers of his school of thinking have shown that if you meditate and pray, even the cholesterol level in the blood will fall. Clearly, there are many healthful physiological consequences of engaging in prayer.

The response to prayer, however, that attracts me goes beyond that intra-personal experience. I am more interested in the effects of prayer on other people. I am fascinated by the fact that even though I may be on one side of the earth and you may be on the other, your prayer for me could change my physiology. That goes far beyond what has been investigated at Harvard and in other places. I think we ought to honour not only the personal effects on an individual who prays, but also the distant effects — what have traditionally been called the intercessory effects of prayer.

To understand the effects of intercession, I believe that we have to go beyond physical explanations. At this point in our knowledge, we have to admit that we don't understand how prayer works. It's acceptable in science to say that you don't know how something works. In medicine, we're often forced to say this. For many years we did not know how penicillin works, for example. Science is very good at showing us *that* a thing works. *How* it works is another question. I think, however, that the explanations are on their way. I'm convinced that some of the hypotheses now being advanced will one day bear fruit.

My personal explanation is theistic, although I think it is valuable to pick a term that is rather neutral in its theological implications. I use the term *The Absolute* instead of *God*. But I think that theologians and other people who wish to bring God into the explanation of the effects of prayer are fully justified in holding their ground. They need not be pushed around by science. In fact, for every question that science answers about the mystery of prayer, it will raise a dozen more that it can't answer. There is no need to worry that science is going to debase prayer. I think it will honour prayer. A famous poll in 1997 showed that 40 per cent of American scientists believe in the kind of God who would answer intercessory prayer.

In our culture it is common to feel forced to choose between being scientific and rational or spiritual and intuitive. Most physicians become analytical and rational, and we call this the scientific path. But these are false options. Choosing one over the other makes a schizophrenic division in our lives that has caused a tremendous amount of pain. One of the great benefits of the data about prayer is that it clearly illustrates that we can have it both ways. We can bring science and spirituality together in our lives, and the result will be healing for physicians and for the whole of society.

If God does respond to prayer, how do we explain why he seems to listen to some prayers and not to others?

I have no answers to this question, nor do I think that science can answer it. We have to rely on our theologians and philosophers to help us understand these matters. However, I have some personal responses. We can look at the glass as either half empty or half full. We can complain that prayer seems not to work all the time or we can be grateful that it does work much of the time. I prefer the latter response. We might say that prayers are always answered. Most of us can see that a prayer is answered when we receive a Yes answer. But No is a perfectly good answer to prayer, even though we may not like it. It's a blessing in disguise that prayer isn't always answered with a Yes. We pray for some of the nuttiest, craziest things, and as C. S. Lewis has warned us, we ought to be grateful that many of those prayers are not answered with a Yes.

Are all kinds of prayer equally effective?

I have a very broad definition of prayer: comunication with The Absolute. This definition is so broad that it infuriates people who want to narrow the definition of prayer to make it sectarian or denominational. But I choose a very broad definition of prayer purposely. Around the earth most people pray, and if we narrow our definition too far, we are disenfranchising most of the world's population who pray differently than we do.

I invite people to define for themselves what communication with The Absolute might look like — what form it might take. It might involve the ritual use of words in formal worship. It might involve the use of silence beyond any kind of image or form or words, of entering what in meditation has been called the void and what in Christian history has often been called contemplation. For most people in our culture, The Absolute takes the form of a personal god, but for an increasing number of people that is no longer true.

I am uncomfortable with the inclination to think that some people pray right and some people pray wrong. I sometimes want to put on my scientist hat and say, "Science can test this." We can take prayer into the laboratory and design experiments in which, for example, people pray that certain bacteria may grow faster than others or that some wounds may heal faster than others. We have invited Muslims, Buddhists, and Christians of all stripes to be the intercessors, and in these experiments we find that religious affiliation makes no difference. All the prayers tested in the laboratory work. People generally respond to this result in one of two ways: those who think they have cornered the market on prayer and believe that God will not answer the prayers of any other group are disturbed. The prayer experiments show that that is bigotry. Others are pleased because the experiments show that prayer belongs to the entire human race. Its efficacy isn't restricted to particular denominations.

One of the most practical questions about prayer is this: if it works, what kind of prayer works best? Two different forms of prayer have been tested in the studies. One form is *directed prayer*. In other words, you direct the outcome of the prayer by praying for something very specific. You pray for a cancer to go away or for a heart attack to be healed. The other form of prayer is *non-directed*. You don't ask for anything specific. Instead you pray, "Thy will be done," or "May the best thing happen in this situation; may the highest good prevail." When these two forms of prayer have been compared in proven studies, they have both been shown to work. I think this shows that we have to honour not only different religions with their different approaches to prayer, but also different strategies for praying. From all these findings we learn the importance of being tolerant about prayer.

The laboratory studies show that some people achieve better effects by their prayer than others. This raises the question of whether or not there's a skill factor in prayer. It seems to me we ought to take this data seriously, but I don't think there is a simple explanation for it. For example, mere years of experience does not make for more effective prayer. If I had to single out one quality that correlates with effective prayer in these tests, it would be love, or compassion, or empathy. I think most people understand this intuitively. Certainly the great healers throughout history have affirmed the role of love in healing. They will say, for example, that if you really want to use prayer to heal someone at a distance, you have to care. You have to feel it in your heart. You can't just perfect cold technique. There has to be some authentic inner experience of love in the prayer if it is to be effective.

Children have a way of making loving, unconditional connections with other people, and for this reason the prayer of children can be very effective. Many of the wisdom traditions, including Christianity, advocate becoming as a child in spiritual maturity, in order to recapture the innocence of the unconditional love and empathy that children often exhibit. If we can do that, I'm convinced that our prayers will be much more powerful than they often are.

Probably we all begin life as natural healers, but some of us honour and develop that gift more than others do. It is the same with other gifts, such as musical ability, which some nurture and develop to a greater extent than most. It may be that some people are prodigies in healing just as some people are prodigies in music.

Can prayer be used to cause negative consequences?

People throughout history have talked about a negative side to human intention and even prayer. Like most individuals in our culture, I was taught that prayer has either a positive effect or none at all. But the laboratory experiments raise a very troubling third possibility; namely, that prayer may be used to cause harm. Some of these experiments showed clearly that prayer can be used to reduce the healing rate of wounds or kill certain types of cells.

I continued to ignore this data until, in 1994, I stumbled upon the results of a Gallup poll that revealed that 5 per cent of Americans actually pray for harm to come to other people. This was the incentive that nudged me into going back and looking at the studies more fully.

In some studies researchers have used actual cell tissue of human beings to see if individuals could harm or even kill those cells by prayer. One of the commonest cells that they have worked with is cervical cancer tissue from women. The results show that, through negative prayer or negative intention, the subjects can actually harm and sometimes kill the cancer tissue. I think this is a great gift. When we pray for someone with an infection, for example, AIDS or serious pneumonia, we are asking for the destruction of those viruses or bacteria that are causing the problem. So the negative aspect of prayer, if used wisely, can be turned into something exceedingly positive.

There is a spectrum of negative prayer. People use it in a great many ways. Perhaps the least serious are the little off-hand curses we make: "Damn him," or "To hell with her." A woman once wrote to me saying that she had been using a lot of negative prayers like these, and she was going to take responsibility for them and stop using them. She understood the connection between negative thoughts and prayers and their possible results, and she cleaned up her thoughts.

At the other end of the spectrum are people who deliberately use prayer to try to kill other people. These people are often extremely religious, and often in their experience, the object of the prayer will die. Does the prayer cause the death? Obviously, we can't study this in the laboratory because it's illegal to do an experiment or a study whose goal is to harm another human being. But since we know from the studies that negative prayer is effective in killing human tissue, we ought to take seriously the possibility that it can kill other people or seriously harm them.

Between the two extremes is a huge grey area in which prayer is used to try to manipulate or control other people so that they follow the agenda of the person praying. One of the ways in which we do this was illustrated to me when I wrote my first book on prayer, *Healing Words*, in 1993. The book drew a lot of interesting letters from people who disagreed with some of the conclusions it set forth. The conclusion that most infuriated people was that when prayer was tested in the laboratory, the prayers of practically any religion worked. Various fundamentalists were enraged by this claim, and some of their letters were dripping with hatred. Invariably these people would say, "We're going to pray for you, Dr. Dossey." My initial response was to thank them, but as I began to think about how they were using prayer, I saw it as a subtle form of manipulation and control. These people were praying that I would come around to their way of thinking. Interestingly, all these prayers were offered in the name of love, but I soon stopped accepting them because manipulation and control are not loving. When I rejected these prayers, I opposed them with prayers of my own that I would be protected against manipulation. I think we often slip into using prayer to manipulate other people and to inflict our wishes on them. We can escape responsibility for doing this by telling ourselves that, if the prayer works, it must be God's will. So prayer is used as a vehicle by a lot of people to lay their selfish trip on somebody else. We always have to be careful when we pray to make sure we're not falling into that trap.

How do you protect yourself from other people's negative influences through their dark prayers or their negative intentions towards you? One of the best antidotes to negative prayer is positive prayer. I live in northern New Mexico, where the Native American tradition is very strong, and this has given me an opportunity to explore methods of protection with Native American healers, who all believe in negative influences. A famous Aboriginal healer asked, "Dr. Dossey, have you ever heard of the Lord's Prayer? Do you remember the clause, 'deliver us from evil'? You white people have one of the most powerful forms of protection going, and you don't even realize it."

Imagery and visualization can be potent forms of protection. Many people tell me that they visualize themselves surrounded by a white light or a thick protective wall, and that this helps them feel protected against the intrusions of other people.

So there are many ways of protecting ourselves from the negative prayers of others. It is possible, however, to be too concerned about the negative effects of other people in our lives. I think we have a psycho-spiritual immune system that works automatically to protect us from the negative thoughts and prayers of other people, much as our physical immune system protects us from infection. If we add periodic prayers, such as "deliver us from evil," most of us don't have to worry a lot about the negative prayers of others.

Are medical "curses" a form of negative prayer?

The health care setting provides many examples of random comments that have the effect of a curse, a hex, or a spell. Every medical doctor knows how serious a prognosis is. When doctors say, for example, "You have six months to live," people can live out this prediction and die as if on cue. This may seem far removed from negative prayer; the doctors aren't actually praying to harm other people and they aren't intentionally trying to kill anyone by their casual comments, but there are a lot of cases on record where patients have died after hearing a negative comment from a physician. The comments may be more subtle. For instance, "This is the worst case of this illness I've ever seen," or "You should have had this surgery last week." Comments like these are sometimes called "truth-dumping" — dumping a statistical truth into the patient's lap. They can function as literal curses, hexes, or spells.

Fortunately, most physicians are becoming more aware of the potential negative impact of these sorts of comments, and there are courses now in most medical schools about doctor-patient communication. I know physicians who can tell patients that they have six months to live in such a way that the patients are filled with hope. These doctors emphasize that not everybody dies in six months; half the people live on and many are even cured of the problem. The effect depends on emphasis and nuance. In order to avoid informing someone in a hurtful way, doctors must have love and compassion and be able to put themselves in the place of the patient. That's what empathy actually is. That's what "bedside manner" used to be about: putting yourself in the place of the patient and seeing how that person is going to respond to what you're about to say. So we come back to the role of empathy, and the role of love, which we've already identified as one of the major factors in the power of prayer. In medicine, if we want to be good physicians, we simply can't run away from the power of love.

Do physicians have an ethical obligation to seek patients' permission to pray for them?

If doctors take seriously the data showing that prayer actually works, they have to ask themselves whether to pray for their patients. At a certain point in my professional life, I answered with a Yes and began to adapt prayer to my work as a physician. In my office early every morning I would have a prayer ritual for the patients I was about to see in the hospital or in my office that day. After a great deal of thinking, I chose to pray in solitude for my patients. I know physicians who think it is their duty to pray at the bedside. This is a legal principle in modern medicine. If a doctor wants to do surgery on a patient, the doctor has to inform the patient of all the potential negative outcomes and side-effects and the patient has to agree in writing to the procedure. Should we obtain informed consent before praying for our patients? It may seem hopelessly legalistic to do so. If prayer works, why not simply pray? The reason is simple: not everybody wants to be prayed for. People have already threatened lawsuits on the grounds that it is an invasion of their privacy and their psychological space to be prayed for. I don't think we're justified in inflicting prayer on people against their will. We ought to give more thought to obtaining permission before we pray for people.

There are situations, however, where it is totally unnecessary to seek permission. For example, in an emergency when someone is unconscious, you obviously cannot get their informed consent before praying for them, nor can you get the informed consent of infants. A way of avoiding all the complications raised by informed consent is to use an open-ended, non-directed form of prayer. If we pray for an individual and simply ask, "Thy will be done," or "May the very best thing happen in this situation," I fail to see why informed consent is necessary. We're not trying to inflict our own personal agenda on anyone if we pray this way, provided that we are guided by love.

Like most people, I grew up thinking that prayer was something you did — an activity associated with certain times of the day, like mealtime or bedtime. Now my prayer is much more diffuse. Prayerfulness is what matters; it's an attitude, a way of being. Someone once tried to pin down Thomas Merton by getting him to describe exactly how he prayed. When Merton replied that he prayed by breathing, he was saying that prayer can permeate an individual. Prayer can suffuse you and direct how you conduct yourself. It can become as natural as breathing. At this point, asking permission to pray is like asking permission to be yourself.

What is the future of prayer in medical practice?

Three years ago only three medical schools in the United States had courses honouring the role of religious devotion and prayer in health. As a result of physicians becoming more aware of the data about prayer and religious practice in healing, today nearly 50 medical schools have courses that focus on these issues. Spirituality is returning to medicine. We have an opportunity here both to re-humanize modern medicine and to help spirituality make friends with science. I hope to continue to be part of this movement. In particular, I want to say more in a future book about the role of love in healing. My interest has grown out of study of the prayer data which suggests that the combination of love with prayer is what brings about the healing.

BELIEF CAN INDUCE HEALING BY EVOKING THE RELAXATION RESPONSE

DR. HERBERT BENSON *is a cardiologist who teaches in the faculty of medicine at Harvard University in Cambridge, Massachusetts.*

What is the relaxation response?

To the extent that any disorder is caused or made worse by stress, it may be effectively treated and even cured by means that generate relaxation. Sixty to 90 per cent of visits to doctors are for stress-related disorders. Stress-related disorders are in the mind-body realm, and they're poorly treated by pharmaceuticals and surgery.

There are degrees of healing. At one end of the spectrum, healing is curing, which is the complete alleviation of the disease state. At the other end of the spectrum, healing is learning to accept the disease. In between, it can involve mental healing that helps to alleviate the physiological symptoms.

We know that certain types of prayer elicit a set of physiological changes in the body. This is especially true with the repetition of certain verbal formulae; for example, "Hail Mary, full of grace"; "The Lord is my shepherd"; "Our Father who art in heaven"; "Om Mani Padma Hum." You repeat the words on each breath, and when other thoughts intrude, you let them go and bring your attention back to the repetition of the words. With the repetition comes a certain set of physiological responses; for example, the rate of metabolism decreases, the heart rate decreases, the rate of breathing decreases, brain waves get slower.

You can repeat any word, prayer, or phrase to achieve the relaxation response. The vast majority of people in the world will use a prayer, but other words will do. Even a repetitive muscular activity that works independently of a belief system is effective in bringing about the physiological changes that can cure a disease, to the extent that it's caused or made worse by stress.

There is however, another component that comes into play: the belief of the patient. When belief is added to the repetition, the relaxation response may be encouraged and strengthened. In medicine, we have made fun of belief. We have so denigrated the power of belief that we call it the placebo effect. "It's all in your head," we say, "There's nothing real about this disease."

What is the role of belief in healing?

Health care is like a three-legged stool held up by one leg of pharmaceuticals, another leg of surgery and related procedures, and a third leg of self-care. Nutrition, exercise, stress-management, and our belief system are all aspects of self-care. The repetition of a verbal formula is another aspect of self-care. We tend to think of medicine as being primarily those first two legs: drugs and surgery. Consequently, we expect health care to be done to us, not by us. But drugs and surgery don't really treat stress-related illnesses; the power of belief, on the other hand, works in the mind-body realm. Of course, it would be unthinkable to do away with penicillin, cataract surgery, and other drugs and procedures that we know are curative, but we need the third leg of self-care to balance the health care stool.

A number of diseases have been shown in medical studies to be responsive to treatment by a placebo, such as a simple sugar pill. Obviously, a placebo such as a sugar pill depends on belief for its effectiveness. For many decades now in medicine, we have carried out studies in which we compare a new drug or procedure against a placebo. If the new pill works no better than the placebo, we throw it out. But we have found from these studies that 50 to 90 per cent of many conditions are improved or completely alleviated by the taking of placebos. These include angina pectoris, asthma, rheumatoid arthritis, duodenal ulcers, all forms of pain, skin rashes, even death itself. A placebo is an example of people's belief helping to heal them.

These same sicknesses or conditions can also be generated or exacerbated by a person's beliefs. Take, for example, the case of an Australian aborigine, eighteen years old, who was told not to eat wild game hen or he would die. He went to a friend's home for some dinner and was given wild game hen, but the friend lied and told him it was something else. He ate it and felt fine. Two years later when he returned, the friend said, "Hah, I tricked you. I gave you wild game hen two years ago when you came to dinner." Within twenty-four hours the young man died. This story reveals to us the power of belief to cause sickness and death. But just as belief can cause them, so it can relieve sickness and keep us alive.

How does belief work? How can it turn on a rash or turn off a rash? Our brains are "wired" in countless trillions upon trillions of connections. Every thought we have, every memory we have, every action we carry out, is "wired" into our brain and becomes part of it. In an experiment done by Dr. Stephen Cosley, people looked at a grid in which there was a capital letter A. As they were staring at the grid with the letter A, he did a PETscan on their brains, and a certain area of the occipital cortex in the back of the brain lit up. At the next stage in the experiment, the subjects looked at a grid in which there was no letter A, but they were instructed to visualize it as being there. When their brains were again scanned, exactly the same area lit up. From the brain's point of view, believing that you are looking at something is the same reality as actually looking at something.

People can turn on all sorts of symptoms in their body by believing in them — rashes, asthma attacks, headaches, pain — because the memories of those symptoms are there within our brains. The switch is in the brain. You just have to say, "Every time I see Aunt Milly, I get an asthma attack" — and you do! You are "wired" for the asthma attack, and you can turn it on.

Now, if you believe that therapy you are receiving will alleviate the asthma attack, the asthma attack will indeed disappear. In fact, in England there have been experiments in which asthmatic patients were told that something in a vaporiser they were given would cause an asthma attack. Even though the vaporiser contained nothing but distilled water, they had an asthma attack. Next they were told told that they were being given something that would alleviate the asthma. Once again, the vaporisers contained only distilled water, but the patients' asthma was alleviated.

Another experiment in England focused on the swelling resulting from the extraction of molar teeth. Some people believed that waving an ultrasonic wand over the area where the tooth was pulled would reduce the swelling. When the wand was waved by a dentist or another person, sometimes it was plugged in and sometimes it was not, but even when it wasn't plugged in, it alleviated swelling. Obviously there was no ultrasound coming out of it. The healing was brought about by the patients' belief. Furthermore, the results were better for the unplugged-in wand, and better when it was waved by a dentist than when it was waved by another person.

Here is another story to illustrate the power of belief. A minister who was allergic to flowers refused to conduct any service — even funerals — if flowers were present. He made it clear that he would go into anaphylactic shock if there were flowers near him, and he could die from it. When he was called to do a certain funeral, he reminded the people that there shouldn't be flowers, and they agreed not to bring any. But a woman showed up with a dozen roses. He developed an anaphylactic reaction and had to be taken to the hospital. Later, when he confronted the woman, she told him they were plastic flowers.

We are all "wired" for the power of belief. The most powerful belief for many people is belief in God. In America, some 95 per cent of people believe in God. Let's assume that you believe in God; you have an illness, that illness is healed, and you attribute the healing to God. Now, from the narrow viewpoint of medicine, whether or not God actually exists makes no difference to the healing. What makes the difference is your belief.

We don't know whether God exists or not. But since so many people have believed in God from the earliest days for which we have a record, we can argue that we are "wired" to believe in God just as we are "wired" to learn to walk, talk, and remember. Still there remains the question: does God exist? Or does our belief that God exists stem from an area of the brain that CATscans have shown produces spiritual feelings — feelings about powers, forces, energies beyond us? From the point of view of medical science, the answer doesn't matter. When that area of the brain is activated, it helps us get better.

If a person relied only on his belief system, however, that would be like trying to hold up the three-legged stool of health care on just one leg. Barbara Dawson was a woman who suffered from cancer and also had very serious heart disease. She refused an operation for cancer because it would be so mutilating. Instead, she put her faith in God and did very well. But she did use radiation and drugs.

It worries me that people might misinterpret our work and give up medicine. Cancer provides a good example. Stress does not cause cancer although stress may influence cancer. To treat cancer you use the whole therapeutic armamentarium. You use surgery, you use radiation, you use chemotherapy, and you also use the belief system. Then, if the cancer continues, you can rest assured that no stone was left unturned, whereas if you rely totally on the belief system and the attempt to cure fails, as doctor or as patient you will be smitten with a sense of failure or guilt.

While we need to balance science with belief, science is necessary to validate when healing occurs and when it can be attributed to belief. I'm a trained cardiologist, and when I saw that meditation evoked the relaxation response and prayer did the same, I felt totally unqualified to explain this phenomenon. It was through science that I came to see the power of belief.

It was also through science that I came to believe that there is an organizing principle to the universe, but it's not necessary to believe even that to be healed. All that is needed is your recognition of the power of belief.

Can intercessory prayer help in healing?

I think the jury is still out on whether prayer for someone other than yourself can work when the people being prayed for don't know they are being prayed for. There are flaws in the studies that have been done, and those studies have to be replicated. We know that belief assists healing, but when the patients don't know that the prayer is going on, our current science cannot explain how prayer may have helped them to get better. Whether healing occurs in those circumstances, I don't know. Conclusive experiments still have to be done.

But belief can heal. Belief can cure. What's important is not what the doctor believes in but what the patient believes in. It's important for doctors to listen to patients and to use the patients' own healing powers along with what we can dispense medically. One way of doing this is to give them a choice of how to elicit the relaxation response. They can use a word, a sound, a prayer, or a phrase. We can ask them whether they would like to use a secular term or a religious one. I think it would be crossing a boundary that should not be crossed if a physician who believed in a certain religion told a patient to use that religion's kind of prayer. If the patients are not religious, I would help them to find words that capture their own belief system — perhaps something about peace or love. If they are religious, they will likely choose words from their own religious tradition that are meaningful to them.

Experiments done at the Massachusetts General Hospital have shown that the death rate of people going into surgery who are not only fearful of death but are convinced they're going to die is 100 per cent. The explanation is not that they lack a belief system to keep them alive, but that they want to die; perhaps to be reunited with a loved one, perhaps to stop being a burden on their families.

We are the most intelligent beings on earth and our intelligence has given us control, for better or for worse, of the entire world. Now, being so intelligent brings its own problems. One is that we know we're mortal. We are the only animal alive that is conscious of its mortality. In a moment of agony, an animal may know it is going to die, but we know from our earliest years that we're going to die. We sometimes ask ourselves, "Why go on? Why have children? Why care about living?" Belief in an after-world gives us hope and that hope gives meaning to our lives. That hope may be how we are "wired" to God, because God is the essence of something more than our mere mortality.

Will the power of belief always remain a mystery? I don't know. Science is getting so good. But I think what will remain a mystery is where the capacities to believe and to use belief in healing came from. Were they derived strictly from evolution because it's good for us to believe? Maybe it was helpful for our evolution to believe that we could overcome suffering and death. On the other hand, one can equally argue that these capacities were placed there by a greater power, force, or energy.

DISTANT HEALING IMPROVES PATIENTS' HEALTH

DR. ELISABETH TARG, *a psychiatrist, is the Director for the Complementary Medicine Research Institute at the California Pacific Medical Center. She served as principal investigator for a large, recently completed research project evaluating the efficacy of distant healing for people with AIDS.*

Will you tell us how you became interested in the effects of prayer in healing?

Our goal at the Complementary Medical Research Institute is to take a long and rigorous scientific look at a variety of complementary and alternative approaches to healing. Years ago, I did research with people with AIDS and HIV to try to understand the role played by their psychological state in the development of their illness or their well-being, especially the imagery that was in their minds. My question was whether intentionality could make a difference to their health.

It was only a short step to asking whether another person's intention for them, expressed for example in prayer, could make a difference to their health. Of course, from a psychiatric point of view, we would expect someone to feel better if a kind, well-intentioned person promises to help them, because we know that mind and expectation have a profound impact upon health and well-being. But I wanted to go beyond that effect to discover whether someone else's *intention* could affect their health.

What experiment did you design to test whether another person could heal someone who is sick by praying for them?

I prefer the more inclusive term *distant healing* to the term *prayer*, because many of those who agreed to work as healers in our experiments would not describe what they are doing as prayer.

We selected as our healers people who had a professional practice in healing, had worked at it for at least five years, had worked at some point with people with HIV, and had in the past worked at a distance. They included Christians, Jews, Buddhists, people from Native North American traditions, and people from secular contemplative schools of healing. They were all deeply compassionate people who volunteered to participate. They all knew that, since we would not be able to validate any one person's healing skills in the experiments, there would be no direct benefit for them; their work would be an act of love.

The patients were all people with advanced AIDS, that is, with T-cell counts under 200 and at least one AIDS-defining illness. In our first study we worked with twenty patients and in the second, with forty. In each study we divided them into two groups with essentially equal levels of illness. Both groups got regular medical treatment. One of the groups got distant healing in addition, and the other was the control group. The healing was done in double-blind fashion; that is, neither the patients nor any of the healers or experimenters knew which patients were in which group. So, if I spoke with a patient in the study, there was no way of my even suggesting that he was lucky to be in the distant healing group.

The healers and the patients never met. The healers were sent photographs, first names, and a little information about each patient. And then, so that we could be sure that we weren't inadvertently testing the skill of one healer or one healing tradition as compared with another, we put the healers on a rotation during the ten weeks of the experiment. Each patient got a one-hour treatment every day for ten weeks, but the treatment would be by a different healer each week.

Over the study period, the distant healing group experienced significantly fewer outpatient doctor visits, fewer hospitalizations, fewer days of hospitalization, fewer new AIDS-defining diseases, and a significantly lower illness severity level.

This result is hard to explain. It has been suggested that the placebo effect comes into play when a patient's improvement occurs as a result of believing in the effectiveness of the treatment. This placebo effect should lead to better outcomes among patients who believe they are in the treatment group, regardless of which group they are actually assigned to. However, in our experiments, differences in medical outcome were related to the true group assignment, not to what patients believed. Existing medical understanding cannot account for distant healing. But Dr. Larry Dossey has pointed out that morphine, aspirin, and quinine were used effectively for years before anyone understood how they work.

I have long been interested in parapsychology. A large number of parapsychological studies show that an individual sitting in a laboratory can accurately describe a place, an object, or an event a long distance away, although there is no apparent means for the person's getting the information about the place, object, or event. If an individual can describe what is happening in London right now, then what is happening in London right now is affecting the individual. Knowing this opens the door to understanding how changes in the consciousness of one person might affect the consciousness — and thereby the physical and emotional well-being — of another person.

You cannot draw firm conclusions from one or two studies. Our work needs to be replicated and looked at from different angles. My interest right now is in opening a dialogue on the subject of distant healing because it seems to be replete with power to do good.

A SCIENTIFIC STUDY RAISES QUESTIONS ABOUT THE QUALITY OF PRAYER

DR. SCOTT WALKER *is Assistant Professor of Psychiatry at the University of New Mexico's Centre on Alcoholism, Substance Abuse, and Addictions.*

∽∽∽

What questions arose from your study of healing prayer?

A number of years ago, the United States National Institute of Health, Office of Alternative Medicine, put out a proposal asking for community-based alternative health care practitioners to collaborate with university-based researchers to examine scientifically what the practitioners were doing. I received a grant to look at intercessory prayer in the treatment of alcohol abuse and dependence. This study took place several years ago and has been recently published in *The Journal of Alternative Therapies*.

One small study doesn't prove anything. It just gives us some hints about directions in this brand-new field of examining spirituality scientifically. Probably the single most striking thing about the research literature in medicine is how much spirituality and prayer have been excluded from consideration as a means of healing. So we don't know yet what the right questions are. The purpose of a small pilot study such as the one we completed is to open up the field, so that we can figure out what we need to look at.

We asked people who were coming voluntarily into a large public alcohol and drug treatment program if they were willing to participate in a study that would look at the value of prayer in healing. They were people with a diagnosis of primary alcohol dependence. Almost nobody refused and almost everybody was very interested. Everybody got regular substance abuse treatment, but about half were randomly assigned to a group who were being prayed for.

The volunteers who would do the praying were recruited initially from an organization called the Albuquerque Faith Initiative, which was trying to educate religious professionals and laity about the problems of substance abuse. We asked for people with a history of praying and some experience with their prayers being answered. They had to be willing not to pray for religious conversion, to maintain confidentiality, and to record daily what they prayed for, throughout a period of six months. Our initial sample of people came from a wide variety of religious backgrounds, but the only people who actually completed the full six months of reporting were Catholics, Protestants, and Jews. Each volunteer got three clients to pray for, and each client got four to six people to pray for them daily. Those praying were asked to record anything unusual that happened in relation to their patients during their prayer time.

At the end of the study, we were not able to demonstrate a difference in alcohol use between the group being prayed for and those not being prayed for. But there was a difference between the groups in the dropout rate. Far more people who had not been prayed for disappeared: we couldn't find them to do the follow-ups. But even this difference didn't quite reach statistical significance.

We asked a variety of other questions. We asked the people involved, "Are you praying for yourself?" Those people who were praying for themselves were drinking much less. The decrease in their drinking was statistically significant at two or three months but not at six months. From this we learned that research into prayer and healing should consider the amount and quality and type of prayer that people are doing for themselves.

We also asked the participants in the research right at the beginning if anybody was already praying for them. About half of them said Yes – mom, significant other, church, or someone else — and about half said No, at least not that they were aware of. The interesting thing was that those people who said somebody was praying for them were drinking significantly more at six months than those who said nobody was praying for them that they were aware of, regardless of whether or not they were prayed for by outside volunteers.

At this point, we can't say what these findings mean, but they do suggest that we need to look at what is going on in people's agenda when they offer prayers. What are their motivations and what are their intentions when they offer prayer? People who have alcohol problems tend to be marginalized and to be surrounded by the emotional reactions of others to their alcohol abuse. Imagine I am an alcoholic related to you and you're praying for me. You know that I have caused dangerous things to happen — motor vehicle accidents, for example. Are there any negative feelings, such as anger, fear, frustration, in your prayers towards me? Do you have any control agenda? Do you want to change me, and control me, and make me do what's right and best? Are you able to pray for my ultimate good without your own personal agenda coming into it?

A lot of other questions are raised about the person receiving prayer. Suppose I'm a drinker, but I don't think I have a problem. I know you're praying for me, and I think you're a judgemental, controlling person who should mind your own business. When you pray for me, can I block the prayer? I don't have a definitive answer, but this is the question for researchers and practitioners: is it possible to block prayer when your agenda and the recipient's agenda are different? Or if the recipient does not believe in prayer?

Consider some other questions. You're praying for me to have a wonderful life, but what if I believe that I am a bad person who deserves punishment? Can you create what some people would call a shame spiral and actually do me harm with your good intentions? I don't know. But questions arise about whether we should ask permission to pray for people or ask what prayers they would like. This shades into a question about the relationship of prayer and free will. Through prayer, can I override your free will, or change what you choose to do? And if I have the power to do that, is that a wise thing to do?

None of these are trivial questions if prayer has power, as I and many other people believe it does. In the United States, surveys have consistently shown that 90 per cent or more of the population pray. How many even consider the possibility that their prayers might have a negative impact in the world? We had better be very careful about our agenda, our motivations, the purity of our hearts, as we pray.

One small study proves nothing, but it raises many questions that I hope people will take seriously and discuss. Although we might have hoped for more positive results, I think that getting people to seriously think about what they're doing when they pray is in itself a positive step.

Part 2

HEALING PRAYER IN PRACTICE

PRAYER IS WORKING WITH THE DIVINE ENERGY TO BRING WHOLENESS TO LIFE

SISTER CONSTANCE JOANNA GEFVERT *is a member of the Sisterhood of St. John the Divine (SSJD), an Anglican religious order founded in 1884. The order has always emphasized teaching and healing and continues to play an important role at St. John's Rehabilitation Hospital in Toronto, which was founded by SSJD. The hospital is now designated as a regional specialty rehabilitation teaching centre within the Ontario health system, and specializes in musculo-skeletal and neurological rehab. Patients who have had complex orthopedic surgery, suffered strokes, undergone amputations, or are recovering from the traumas of automobile accidents are taught to walk again, to use artificial limbs, to adjust to an altered lifestyle, and to return to as active a life as possible. All this is done in a mult-faith context, with the support of ongoing prayer and special services of healing in the sisters' chapel at the heart of the hospital.*

What is the role of prayer in the healing process?

St. John's is very much a multi-cultural, multi-faith hospital, and we have a very active chapel life. The sisters pray the Divine Office daily, but the chapel is open to many other faith groups, not all of them Christian. In our pastoral ministry at the hospital, we try to be open to a multi-faith dimension, and we see ourselves as offering a ministry of hospitality to all people who come, just as we do at the main convent or any of our other houses. As Christians, we believe that we are called to hasten the coming of the reign of God among us to bring justice and peace to our world. That call applies in all of our ministries, including health care. It means that we must minister to everybody, and not necessarily convert them to Christianity. The gifts of prayer and love and physical healing that God has given us, we try to share with everybody.

Our faith, however, comes to bear in the work we do because we are a community committed to prayer as our first work. We pray for people who cannot pray for themselves, who don't want to pray, who are afraid to pray, who are too tired or sick or hungry to pray, who have never learned to pray. Prayer is at the heart of the healing ministry, and people who are not praying, whether they're the patients or the doctors, nurses, and therapists who care for them, are all supported and energized by the prayer of other people. I don't think God's love is given exclusively to those people who are specifically conscious of God; it is here in the world for all of us to draw upon. SSJD's rule of life says that prayer releases energy into the world for the accomplishment of God's purpose. That's why we pray. So I believe that everybody in a hospital is helped by the prayer of the sisters, whether they are conscious of it or not.

God desires wholeness, reconciliation, and unity for each individual person and for the entire creation. Everything we can do to help bring that about — to be instruments of God's love and peace and healing in the world — is prayer. That may mean a liturgy in the chapel in which we praise God and pray for people who are in need. It may be sitting and talking at somebody's bedside. It may be holding somebody's hand. It may be encouraging family members who are concerned about someone in their family who is ill or who is having to adjust to a new lifestyle. All of these are part of prayer. Prayer is moving with God instead of working against the purposes that God has for creation.

But on a more personal level, prayer is the way we connect with the God who loves us. God is the creator of the universe, but God also has a very personal way of relating to each of us.

Sitting quietly and simply being aware of God's presence with us is a form of prayer. So is reading and reflecting on the scriptures. By these means we connect with the God who created us out of love and who continues to love us and call us into an intimate personal relationship. Even when you're not interceding for someone — praying for somebody's healing, for example — but when you're just being there in a relationship with God, such prayer releases the divine energy, which can be used for God's purposes. And that means healing, wholeness, reconciliation.

For me, some of the traditional Celtic prayers capture best the sense of Christ's healing presence that prayer invokes. In "St Patrick's Breastplate" there is a verse that calls to "Christ within me, Christ behind me, Christ before me, Christ beside me, ... Christ beneath me, Christ above me, ... Christ in hearts of all that love me, Christ in mouth of friend and stranger." This verse describes the sense of God being everywhere in a way that only poetry can; it provides an understanding of God that can't be put into theological categories.

Theology is a way of putting into intellectual categories our understanding of God. Prayer is getting to know God as opposed to getting to know about God. Theology is restricted to the categories of our language. Prayer, like poetry, allows us to break bounds and get a sense of something much bigger. We need our theology to keep us grounded. We need our spirituality to live out our relationship with God. Our spirituality includes prayer, our relationship with other people, what we do about the environment and about political situations — everything that is the living out of our faith. Intellectual understanding and spirituality have to go together.

Prayer takes practice. It requires learning to focus. A photographer knows that you can set a camera to give more or less depth of field. With greater depth of field, objects at varying distances are all in focus. In prayer, if you have a great depth of field, you're going to be aware of people walking in and out of a room, of cars tooting their horns outside, of birds singing, and of all the noise going on in your own mind. But just as you can focus the camera lens to get a very narrow depth of field, so in prayer you can focus on God and let all the rest go out of focus in the background. Learning to do this requires practice. I find that if I try to fight the distractions, they become more distracting and I become focused on them. It is as if I've shifted the camera away from the flower I'm photographing to part of the background. So I try to accept that all of the things I think about, worry about, or am aware of are parts of the life that God has given me; then I give thanks for them and return my focus to God.

Sometimes, however, when distracting thoughts keep coming into our minds when we're trying to pray, God is bringing to our awareness someone that we need to pray for, or something that we've been avoiding thinking about. In very quiet centring prayer, material comes up from the unconscious that our busy lives allow us to keep suppressed, and it demands a response from us. Sometimes a person keeps coming to mind. If you are a workaholic, for example, and your spouse or children keep coming to mind, maybe God is telling you that they are crying for some attention from you. Since God works through our unconscious, you always have to be discerning about the distractions that arise in prayer.

How would you define healing?

God has created a world that was intended for wholeness, but for various reasons it is broken. There is brokenness in our organizational lives, in our national lives, in our international lives, and in our personal lives as well. And yet, because of the way we're created, there is something within us that is always driving us towards wholeness and reconciliation within ourselves, with other people, and with the whole creation. Now, the kind of healing that we need is not always apparent to us. While we pray for healing, we have to leave it to God, who best knows what we need, to determine what the healing will be. It may be healing a physical disease, a relationship, or something much deeper inside the person. The only legitimate way we can pray for healing is to ask for what God knows requires healing in that person.

Sometimes ending a relationship is the way to healing when the relationship itself can't be healed. Other relationships may be healed and continue. For some people, healing may come at the time of their death. If you come from a religious tradition that believes death to be a natural part of our life, then death is not always the worst thing that can happen. We've all seen amazing things happen to families when someone is dying, and at the bedside, old antagonisms are healed. This may have a much more profound influence on the next generation than the dying person's physical healing might have had.

I believe very strongly that God always works in cooperation with us when we are open to the divine energy. God is always working for healing — but not necessarily the healing that we expect.

What do you think of the studies showing that people heal better and faster if they are prayed for?

You know what it's like if you're trying to dance with a partner who's going off in one direction and you're going off in another. You don't get anywhere, it's not fun, it's just a fight. But if you're dancing with someone who's moving to the music the way you are, real creativity comes out of that dance. It's like that with God. When people are in concert with God's energy and working with God rather than against God, wonderful things happen.

But there is so much creative energy in the world that we'll never be able to explain it completely. If we think of God's creation as a great umbrella that we stand under, we can never understand it from underneath, so to speak, because we can't see the top of it. If an airplane crashes, I can never answer the question, "Why did that person die and this one live?" Perhaps there was no reason except where they happened to be sitting in the plane. I don't think God predetermines every moment of our lives, including the means and moment of death. I think that, since God has left the creation free, there are many natural and human-made forces that create disasters.

So it's fine to do experiments on the power of prayer, but we have known for a long time that people who are prayed for are more likely to be healed than those who aren't, without scientists trying to demonstrate it. Although we'll never be able to explain it fully, it's easy to understand when you think about the energy that arises when people work together instead of at odds with one another. There is an energy for healing in the world. When we pray for people — even if they don't know we're praying — we are helping to tap into that energy and make it flow in a way that it can't when we're not praying. How exactly that happens, I don't know.

HEALER AND PATIENT COOPERATE IN IMAGING WHOLENESS

EETLA SORACCO *is a spiritual healer living in New Mexico.*

How did you become a healer?

It's a long story. I always wanted to become a doctor. I worked as an operating room nurse on the Russian front during the Second World War. When I came to America I worked for five doctors as a physiotherapist, and then I began medical training with the doctors' encouragement. Just at that point, I developed a terminal brain tumour and was given about a month to live. Thirty years ago it was impossible to operate on a tumour in the pituitary gland, so I was sent home to die. I felt that death was very close, but I wanted to know before I died what my purpose in life was. Immediately, death withdrew a little. Next day a friend came to visit and offered to take me to a psychic healer at a church close by. I said, "My dear friend, I'm dying, can't you see? I cannot go any place. Even getting dressed causes terrible stress." But she threw some clothes on me and took me to that church where a Reverend Rosalyn Bruyere was talking about auras and energy fields and communicating with dead people. As a pre-medical student I thought what nonsense this was — hocus pocus — but my friend made an appointment for me with the Reverend Bruyere, who said she felt I was a natural healer and invited me to study with her. I got myself dressed and went to her place and she started healing me and also teaching me.

One day when I was getting ready to see her again, I was so ill I couldn't even brush my teeth or comb my hair, and that made me so angry that I decided to show them all — the doctors and healers — how stupid they were by healing myself. That started the healing process: my own decision to focus on getting well instead of giving my entire attention to my pain and sickness and death. I started changing my attitude towards myself, and I was soon assisting the Reverend Bruyere in her healing work. Before long, I was doing it on my own.

Most of the people that I treat have a very negative attitude towards themselves. I have come to recognize through my own experience that the first step in healing is to change your self-image. When I was in Estonia, I had a very good self-image. I had loving parents, and it was a very supportive society. All this was lost in the war and through immigration to the United States. Americans all seemed beautiful, tall, well dressed, and self-assured, and we were just poor immigrants who had no money, didn't speak the language, didn't know anything. I no longer felt good about myself. At that moment when I decided to get well, I knew that, no matter how short or tall I was or whether I spoke the language or not, I had to be in touch with myself:

With my clients, I'm trying to help them to get in touch with themselves and to love themselves. I ask them to make certain affirmations. I want them to concentrate on their good points. I ask them to write out a list of their positive character- istics and put it in their bathroom, in their bedroom — wherever they are — so that every day they will reaffirm how good they are and all the wonderful things they have done. I also ask them to make a list of the incomplete issues — things they have not yet managed or haven't tackled yet. That list they put into a drawer, leave it alone, and maybe in a month or two, take it out and see how many things they can cross off. I believe in encouraging people by my attitude towards them, but they also have to do their part to gain a kind of connection with their own selves.

I try to go to the root cause of an ailment. For instance, some big happening in your life can cause negative energies to work for years, almost without your noticing them until they finally make you so weak that they take over your whole body. I try to help you go back to what happened. Maybe as a child you were punished when you didn't deserve it and that stuck with you until it weakened you. Through counselling and other tech- niques, I help people to understand that they can participate in their own healing.

I think that we all have the gift of healing. Think of a little boy who has hurt his knee. His mother gives him a kiss, and he feels better. When you're in trouble, and you come to me, my presence and willingness to share your grief helps to heal you.

I believe we all can do this. What it takes is concentration, focus, and intent. The intent is the most important thing. It is the key to healing. We have to want to heal the person and dedicate energy to the process of healing. It is very important, however, to be completely clear of prejudices or judgements when you undertake the healing.

I have always considered myself as a bridge between medical science and metaphysical healing. My background was science and medicine. I would like to help science and medicine to see the good sides of alternative therapies, so that they could work hand in hand. I work with doctors and send my clients to see them. The doctors find that when their patients come to me it is easier to treat them because the patients are more open. They don't need as many medications, and they get better sooner.

Can healing be done at a distance from the person being healed?

A study was done in which AIDS patients in San Francisco were prayed for by people at a distance. We people praying were from all faiths — Protestants, Catholics, Hindus — or none. We directed our thoughts towards particular patients. We were given a picture of the patient and told their first names. We knew the patients had AIDS, but we didn't know where they were; some were not even in San Francisco. The point of the study was to see whether the prayer made a difference even though it was taking place at a distance from the patients.

I took the picture and focused on the man, and I could even hear his thoughts and know whether he was angry or happy. It was better than a telephone conversation. The study was finished last year, and it showed that prayer made a difference. We were surprised, but you can't dispute a scientific study like that.

Nobody knows for sure how it happens. Maybe there is a transfer of energy by means of thought. I think somebody has somehow figured out that a thought can circle the earth in the blink of a eye. You know the experience when somebody calls you on the phone at the very moment you had been intending to call them? — the distance apparently didn't stop the thought from travelling.

I believe that we are all part of God, or whatever higher power there is. All the energy and power comes from this higher source. I believe that we have to be connected to this higher source before we begin the work of healing, and that I am just a channel, a medium. So, when I start with my clients, I always say a prayer; then I direct the energy to the patient's highest good, although I cannot always know what that highest good is.

Why does it work sometimes and not others?

That is a big question that I'm now studying. Some clients who have a very rare disease or one that is known to be very hard to treat feel like celebrities. They say, "I'm a very tough case, you know," almost as if they mean, "See what I have been able to create? — a disease that nobody has ever heard of!" They feel very important because people come and poke them and interview them and write them up in medical journals. Then there are other clients who are feisty: they want to have a fight with you. It's as if they are saying, "Prove to me that you are really a healer. I'll give you something that you cannot handle." In my own case, when I was sick with the brain tumour, I had decided to die because all the experiences of war, losing my home, and being just a poor immigrant weren't really my cup of tea. I had a conversation with the Lord: "I don't even believe you exist anymore because you have caused me so many problems, but if you do exist, I want you to know that I cannot take it anymore." That was almost an unconscious death wish. I think many people who have gone through difficult experiences have made an unconscious death wish. It is very difficult to heal them if they are not ready to receive healing. Healing needs to be a cooperative venture.

I have received many letters from mothers concerning their children, especially sons, who are on drugs or alcohol. They tell me that the entire community has been praying for the son and he's getting worse. I think that this son has an issue with himself. He does not really want to be healed; he's comfortable as he is. When I start working with people, I always ask, "Is it permissible to heal you?" For people to be healed, they have to take responsibility for themselves. It is easier to stay in bed and have somebody else take care of you than to get up and make decisions about what to buy at the supermarket, who to call, how to conduct your business, and how to carry on your life.

Can prayer be used to cause harmful effects?

I have personally experienced the effects of negative prayers. The ancients used to believe in the evil eye. It is still with us. Sometimes if I'm wearing a beautiful dress, somebody will compliment it, but their eyes are full of envy. The next thing that happens is that somebody else spills their food in my lap or my dress catches on a nail and gets ripped. In voodoo you put all your hatred into evil thoughts and energy with negative intentions and send it out across a distance. And it works. Even when people send me letters telling me their troubles, I notice a heaviness on me. In our field these experiences are called psychic attacks. They can be very harsh and can even cause physical ailments. Now of course I have learned to handle them by cleansing myself and turning the heaviness around to make it positive and good.

When I started as a young healer, I was very open-hearted. If you told me a sad story, I would cry and feel miserable with you. But then I wondered, "Who is going to help now that we are both depressed?" I've changed what I do. Now I prepare myself with breathing exercises that fill me with energy, so that I'm on the output; I'm not a sponge. I bring in the breath — the prajna, the life energy — with intention and focus. This activates all the chakras, so they give out energy that creates an aura, is a natural shield to protect me from viruses and pollution and all kinds of negativity. Then when I listen to your story with compassion, I don't become involved to such an extent that I weaken myself. Some healers wear talismans such as certain kinds of stones. I use amber, which gives me a nice glow and reminds me to keep my energy field intact.

ROPING IN THE BABY

DR. BARBARA HANKE, *an emergency room physician in Santa Fe, New Mexico, consulted with Eetla Soracco as a client.*

What circumstances led you, a medical doctor, to see a practitioner who uses non-traditional healing techniques?

I was having problems getting pregnant, staying pregnant, and remaining healthy during pregnancy. It's not hard to recognize when something is glaringly unsuccessful, as was the straightforward medical approach to these infertility issues for me. None of the medical procedures were working. Eetla made me analyze the way I viewed pregnancy in relation to my busy, stressful life. I was trying to compartmentalize the pregnancy, to keep it separate from all the things in my life that were unhealthy, stressful, or non-supportive. She taught me to maintain communication with the baby during the entire pregnancy, beginning with communication with the soul of the child before actually becoming pregnant. Although this is controversial, it is better than just waiting until your ovulation period and hoping the sperm will meet the egg.

We have been working together for about eight years. Through three or four miscarriages, she taught me not to be a passive recipient of fate but to communicate with what was happening. The day I conceived was a medically inopportune day, yet as soon as I conceived, we knew that this pregnancy would go perfectly well. By then I had come to understand the importance of process instead of just going for results. The next day we sent my four-year-old son outside to throw a rope up into the clouds as though he were trying to rope his new brother and bring him down, so we could invite him into the family. Both he and his younger brother still believe that it worked! It's a good visual analogue of what happened through my work with Eetla.

During the pregnancy, whenever I was having a very stressful day in the emergency room and I didn't want the baby to be stressed, it was easy to fall into the illusion that I was strong and protecting the baby. Of course, it doesn't work that way: everything gets through to the baby. I learned to communicate with the baby, saying, "This may seem like a stressful time, but it's okay really; I'm working with these people to help them. I know you are feeling some stress, but this is all right." It turned out to be an easy pregnancy — even delightful.

What was the role of prayer in all this?

I believe there is a higher power that we communicate with even though it isn't tangible. Eelta got me to voice my requests and figure out what I wanted to happen and at the same time to understand that maybe it wasn't going to happen. That was my version of prayer: to ask that certain things would happen if they were right. So I asked for another child if there was a child "out there" who wanted to come and be with our family, but I added that if things didn't work out that way, I could understand it. I think those are elements of prayer.

I pray for my own patients, too, and I encourage their family to pray for them if they're comfortable doing so. I try not to impose additional burdens on the patients or their family by asking them to pray if they don't feel comfortable about it. A lot of the patients I see in the emergency room are critically ill, and they're not necessarily in a position to pray for themselves, but I think they're tuned into what is going on around them, including the prayers. I ask the patients to visualize being very calm and to concentrate on the good things they want to happen, and I touch them more than I used to because I think touch is therapeutic.

More and more, alternative therapists and traditional allopathic physicians are meeting and talking. At St. Vincent Hospital here in Santa Fe, people from the Institute of Medicine and Prayer regularly participate in cancer treatment, and there is a newsletter called *Medicine and Prayer*, which has a wide circulation among medical students and practitioners. I feel that you can take what you need from both Western medicine and spirituality, and that they are not mutually exclusive. In fact, they work better together than either of them works apart.

GOD'S POWER TO HEAL IS FELT IN THE POWER OF LOVE

TERESA ARDANAZ, *a Toronto mother of two, was diagnosed with cancer and attributes its remission in part to the healing power of prayer.*

Can you describe life before and life after receiving the diagnosis of cancer?

We were born in Spain, and therefore I was baptized as a Catholic and received first communion. But I have never been a practising Catholic. I consider myself an agnostic. I do have a sense of God, or something beyond ourselves, and I do feel, on a beautiful day like this, for example, that there has to be something more than we see. I did feel grateful for a very good life overall. But that was really the extent of it before I became ill. I was not a prayerful person, although sometimes I did pray. I would say my sister is the only person in the whole family who has been in any way formal with her religion.

I was leading a very active life, with full-time work and two children, and did not feel ill. Then last April and May I started getting a pain in my side, and it would not go away. I knew that something was seriously wrong. Eventually, a bone scan and a CATscan revealed numerous tumours, and they were obviously secondary to a primary cancer somewhere. A mammogram found the left breast primary tumour, and by then, of course the cancer was in my left lung and bones. So in just a week I went from being, as I thought, perfectly healthy to being a Stage Four cancer case. The chemotherapy treatment was very, very difficult to take — very devastating. Losing all my hair was very hard to take, too. But I now go to a support group at Wellspring and, interestingly, at least 50 per cent of the women there have had the same experience. They had no previous history of cancer, and then they suddenly discovered that they had it seriously.

Can you explain what happened when people began to pray for you?

My sister, the religious member of the family, works for the Anglican newspaper at Anglican Church House, and she therefore has a lot of connections with religious persons. So they immediately started including me in prayers. Soon everybody found out what was going on, and I started getting cards from the places where I worked, saying, "I've included you in a prayer group." One of my ex-teachers wrote to say that she had sent the information to the Sisters of Mercy in

Ireland and they were putting me in their prayers. Within a matter of weeks I was being prayed for by Catholics, Anglicans, Muslims, Jews. We kind of covered all the bases; whichever God is out there was really hearing about what was happening here.

I believe that made a difference to the way I was feeling. During the chemotherapy I spent a lot of time sitting in the room upstairs. I tried to reduce the cancers by visualizing them getting smaller and using all of those visualizing techniques that therapists suggest. Together with that comes prayer, and so I prayed the rosary, which I had never done before. Just reciting the prayers takes your attention off what is happening.

The fact that the tumours are now reducing is really unusual. It is not typical of Stage Four. The conventional chemotherapy and the drug that I am on may be playing a part. Of course, I also take naturopathic and homeopathic medicines and teas. And we have this prayer going on as well. So I'm not entirely sure what combination of things is working. But something is working because the tumours appear to have reduced and I feel so much better. My level of energy compared to five months ago is incredibly higher, and I am reducing the morphine doses over time.

Through a friend of a friend I was connected to a spiritual healer in New Mexico, a Catholic priest. He did a healing prayer over the phone for me on a Sunday night, and coincidentally or otherwise, the following Thursday was the first time that the tumours appeared to have reduced. Two years ago I might have found it almost laughable to think that there could be a connection, but when it happened, it was very real and very moving. I've been keeping in touch with this man, and he is willing to continue to say prayers over me. I'm certainly taking it seriously. He has taught me that you should try to reach the level of faith when you say, "I'm putting myself in your hands, Lord, and I expect to be well." I haven't reached that level yet, of course, because I'm still haunted by the fact that the statistics are against me. But the better I feel, the more positive my frame of mind.

Do you think that God has actually intervened to heal you?

I can't imagine the arrogance of thinking that God actually intervenes in that direct a fashion, saying "You will live — you will die." I think there is an overall framework to a particular life. I think that the desire to live gives one a certain strength and that desire to live may be in some way God-related. But the strength to live isn't just the result of wanting another year of life. It results from loving people. I have not been allowed to feel defeated because family and friends have given massive support. Friends become friends on a completely different level when they are totally involved in the experience. I don't know whether there will be a full recovery with no tumours, but I believe I'll be able to live a longer and better life. This speaks to me of a power of love that has to be related to God. So although I don't see God healing people, I certainly do see that the power of love plays a real part in making you well or making you better.

THE SPIRITUAL EXERCISES OF ST. IGNATIUS OF LOYOLA HAVE HEALING POWER

JOHN WICKHAM, *SJ, a Roman Catholic priest, is Director of the Ignation Spirituality Centre in Montreal.*

Will you please give us a short description of the Ignatian exercises?

St. Ignatius of Loyola, who lived in the sixteenth century and had an unusual gift for spirituality, developed a way of meditating, which he set down in writing and made available to others. It took him about seven to ten years to develop these spiritual exercises. They assume that the person undertaking them wants to convert a life of fairly good habits into a life of total commitment to the service of Christ in this world.

If you go to retreat house, the exercises take a full thirty days of five hours of prayer a day. For working people, we have developed a version in which people pray every day, beginning with thirty minutes a day and working up to about an hour, and they keep a daily prayer journal. Once a week for each of the thirty weeks they come with their prayer journal to see their spiritual director.

The method of prayer is fairly simple. First, you begin by relaxing. You establish a psychic distance between yourself and all the interests of the day.

Second, you turn off the five senses and centre in your heart, not your head. Unlike the conscious mind, the heart is not controlled, and when you identify with the heart, you enter the depths of your being. The heart is like a reception room, and when the Lord knocks on the door — "Behold I stand at the door and knock" — you open and let him in. "Whenever you pray," says the Lord, "go into a room and close the door, and in secret your Father will reward you." It's essential to become very, very interior and to be at peace, dwelling in your heart.

Third, in your imagination you step into the presence of God. There are many ways of doing that and we spend a lot of time teaching these ways to people.

These three steps are really one: you establish a distance from your day in order to be interiorly united with the Lord present to you.

Next, you take a familiar text from scripture and read it over several times. You wait to see what it has to say to you. It will yield all kinds of meaning and experiences when you are in the divine presence, and these you record in your prayer journal for later discussion with your spiritual director. I should emphasize the importance of having a spiritual director.

Can these exercises be used for healing?

L et me give you an example. When I was about twenty-seven, not yet ordained, I felt continually discouraged, as though I would never measure up. I was meditating on Psalm 51, the famous penitential psalm. In this kind of meditation, the idea is to focus on some words that hold your attention, and say them over and over, waiting for something to happen. You don't will it to happen; you wait until it does. So I was looking at the words, "a broken and a contrite heart, O God, shalt thou not despise." It was the word despise that held my attention. Suddenly I recognized that I despised myself and I didn't know why.

The next step was to look away from myself to the Lord, and I understood then that the Lord did not despise. That healing experience cut through habitual attitudes and negative feelings and helped me to get free of them.

LOVING ACTION
IS TRUE PRAYER

PAULINE BRADBROOK *is a theological educator living in Toronto and an active member of the Anglican Church.*

∾∾∾

Can you describe how you have coped with the crisis of the past few months?

It was very, very hard. Three months ago a routine mammogram showed that there was almost certainly a malignancy, and this led to a mastectomy exactly three weeks ago today. One of the hardest things to deal with was the long gaps between seeing health professionals. Sometimes there was a two- or three-week wait for test results, and meanwhile my life was hanging in the balance. I had to find ways to empower myself because it felt as if all the power had been taken away. I think that figuring out how to take back some control had profound benefits for my recovery.

I began to read huge amounts of material on cancer to understand how other women had coped. I visited the Wellspring Centre here in Toronto, where they help men and women with all kinds of cancers get support and information. One of the things that happens with any serious diagnosis of illness is a fragmentation of being. There was a specialist for breast cancer, a specialist for my thyroid condition, the radiologist, and my family doctor, who was removed from this circle. Suddenly I felt like a collection of parts and wondered who was seeing me as a whole person with all the emotional stuff that comes with a cancer diagnosis. That fragmentation felt very disempowering, but I had the feeling that the good naturopathic physician I found was holding all the pieces together, including issues of diet and psychological well-being. That gave me a strong feeling of being able to change how I had been living, particularly by eating more healthfully and trying herbal remedies. I found a massage therapist, who is also a registered nurse, but her work wasn't only with the body; it was also spiritual work because she's a counsellor in addition to all her other skills. Beyond all this, there was an extraordinary outpouring of support from my colleagues at work and people at my church. It was a very lonely journey, but I can't imagine how I would have got through it without that circle of support.

What part has prayer played in helping your healing?

I understand faith as a holistic attitude that approaches life with affirmation. From the moment of our birth we're on a journey to death, though we don't know where or how death is going to meet us. It may come while we're having a meal or crossing the street or dealing with a disease like cancer; there's no way of knowing. Although my faith in God was not shaken, what was shaken was my faith in my own personal strength to live this through. I'm a theological educator, and I'm very aware of all the questions this experience raises about the meaning of life and lives cut short.

A lot of people said they were praying for me. I haven't asked them exactly what that meant — whether it was formal prayer or meditative prayer or something else. I don't know the content of their prayers either — whether they prayed for strength for me or for a good outcome or a cure. But I do know that many, many people said they were praying for me. My own approach to prayer is both formal and informal. I'm an Anglican, and I attend the eucharist weekly. There were times in formal worship when certain prayers simply broke me down emotionally, so I built guards around myself for privacy because I didn't want everyone to know what I was going through. It was only on Easter Sunday that I told the whole congregation that I was going to be having surgery three days later. Consequently, I avoided the usual anointing that we do when members of our congregation are approaching serious surgery.

I continued to work through that three months and my co-workers were incredibly prayerful, but not in a formal way. They just inundated me with flowers and gifts and really funny cartoons. I consider all of that prayer; every gift, every approach, every touch.

My own personal prayer was tuning into that collective love and faith and holding onto it, knowing that it represented ultimate care. I found God's care through the care of friends and community. I don't know if I prayed formally for myself. I can't remember praying for anything other than strength. I lit candles, I burned incense, but as for articulating formal prayers for myself, I don't think I did.

Because of cutbacks to hospital funding in Ontario, I was discharged from the hospital exactly twenty-four hours after the surgery. I walked out of the hospital with the drains still in and, a single woman, I went home. Hundreds of women are being discharged the next day after massive surgery to deal with the physical and emotional impact of it at home. I was blessed in having an incredible team of friends who committed themselves to my never being alone in the house if I didn't want to be, and to providing meals, or cooking, and/or just sitting with me. This was a form of prayer, too. Physically making yourself available in a time of trouble is prayer in its most essential form. It surrounds the suffering person in a spiritual envelope of strength. There was one friend who never uttered a word of anything that would resemble prayer, but she would help me to empty the containers and milk the drains and stay with me while the dressings were renewed. (In that first week I couldn't bring myself to look at the wound.) Caring action like this is certainly a prayer.

I was completely surrounded by all kinds of prayer, and I haven't any doubt that the energy created by the intention of all this prayer buoyed me up and sustained me.

Would you say, then, that you have been healed?

The medical prognosis is good, but learning what that means has required a huge readjustment after three months of a very difficult journey. Yet if I knew that my journey were leading to death from cancer, I would still say that I was being healed in the process.

Healing is not necessarily a miraculous cure; healing is a movement towards wholeness. Wholeness doesn't mean that I will ever get my breast back. The word healing is related to holiness, and it means learning to live in a holy state with whatever the condition is. A spiritual life lived well encompasses the whole of one's being, including finding ways to live with pain or the loss of a limb or an unfavourable prognosis.

For me, also, it means that I have been given a chance to do something new. Many women leave hospital and go home to circumstances very different from the support I had. Growing out of my experience is a desire to make myself available to walk this path with other women. It is already fundamentally reshaping various aspects of my theology, which is very much based on experience, and so it will be useful in the ongoing task of theological education. Too many good, helpful, holy people die tragically and prematurely for me to believe that I've been spared in order to do something helpful. But how to live my life well and usefully in the time before death comes is what my faith is now about.

Part 3

THE HEALING
COMMUNITY

Burrswood:
A Christian
Healing Centre

The following four contributors have all been profoundly affected by their experiences at Burrswood, a Christian healing centre in England. A beautiful, big house set on 290 acres in the green, pastoral English countryside, it is part hospital, part retreat house, part counselling centre. It was founded in 1948 by Dorothy Kerin, who had experienced a miraculous healing, after which God spoke to her in a dream and directed her to heal the sick, comfort the sorrowing, and give faith to the faithless. Her response was to open a house of healing, and from it Burrswood developed. The setting helps; the gardens, the attractive furnishings, the fresh flowers in every room. "The minute you walk in," says Wendy Dimmock, a registered nurse and lay healer, "you feel that love and care and peace fill the place. You feel the presence of Jesus."

Although Burrswood is an Anglican foundation, it admits people from any faith or none. The patients may have had major surgery, or be suffering from a life-threatening disease, or have conditions such as depression or chronic fatigue syndrome. They are of all ages, and include many children. Their illness serves as an opportunity for them to step aside from the busyness of life and examine themselves and their lives with the assistance of professionals from many specialties. "Often," says Dr. Gareth Tuckwell, a medical director at Burrswood, "they use the opportunity to share things that have been in their hearts for years."

The staff includes two priests, doctors, counsellors, nurses, and physiotherapists. They meet as teams with the patients in the thirty-five-bed hospital to work out the best care for them. Michael Fulljames, one of the two priests at Burrswood, explains that an effort is made "to look at the whole person, to try to meet their needs on many levels, to show them care and compassion in the name of God." Four times a week, often in the little wooden chapel on the grounds, there is a healing service with the laying on of hands.

As Wendy Dimmock says, "Christian healing is not just about physical cure and getting better and not hurting. It's about living with the pain and suffering that life inevitably brings."

Michael Fulljames concurs: "Sometimes there is physical healing, and sometimes the healing is in the emotions, and sometimes people receive the strength and grace to cope with pain and trouble and day-by-day problems."

"At the heart of it," says Dr. Gareth Tuckwell, "is God's love at work changing people's lives."

Miriam Dobell, a remarkable Canadian lady, experienced a miraculous healing of her own at Burrswood, and later she was put in charge of a healing ministry in the Diocese of Toronto. When she died, she directed that money from her estate be put towards establishing a similar centre in Canada. With the support of Bishop Terence Finlay, a team of people was selected to undertake the work, including doctors, nurses, priests, counsellors, therapists, administrators, and a lawyer. The team, including Anglican priest Trevor Denny, visited Burrswood and are currently working on garnering support for the project. Among their other investigations, they are seeking an appropriate place in the countryside and working to establish secure financial support.

Both Medical Science and Prayer Contribute to the Wonder of Healing

Dr. Gareth Tuckwell *is a doctor on the staff of Burrswood and Director of the Dorothy Kerin Trust, which administers it. A member of the Pentecostal Church, he is serving on the Archbishops' Commission to review the ministry of healing in the United Kingdom.*

Can prayer bring about miraculous cures?

It's difficult to combine science with spiritual understanding, but here at Burrswood the relationship is very relaxed and easy between the two. It has been said that, where life has no meaning, there is spiritual pain. I believe that spiritual pain often manifests itself in illness. Since ill people are very vulnerable, our purpose at Burrswood is not to impose what we believe on them, but our patients are often glad to share something of their life's journey, and that often provides the key to their illness that opens the door to healing.

Healing helps us to be how God wants us to be in body, mind, spirit, emotions, and relationships. Curing is a physical process. Healing involves the whole of ourselves, our families, our relationships, our whole being.

We are learning that medicine is more than science, that we don't understand it all, and that much of healing is a mystery. Maybe one day we will understand how prayer brings hope and hope brings healing. I believe that the power and presence of Jesus is the key to the mystery and that his healing touch causes the love of God to break through people's illness and despair.

I have witnessed things I can't explain as a doctor. The word *miracle* comes from the Latin *mirare,* which means *to wonder at.* A miracle is something that points to God and causes us to wonder. If our minds are not closed to God but are open to the wonderment of God, then we'll begin to see that there are many miracles around us if our eyes are open to see them.

I can tell you of a miracle. It was a turning point, where we discovered as a family the incredible power of prayer in our own lives. Our son Paul was six months old and was teething. A week before Christmas, at four in the morning, I got up because he was crying and, carrying him downstairs in the dark, I tripped over some books and he hit his head badly. A couple of hours later, he was very pale and began to be sick. We took him to hospital, and by the time the pediatrician had come, Paul was paralyzed down one side and his eyes were fixed. The doctor rang the children's hospital in Great Ormond Street, and they took him with blue flashing lights all the way up to London. He was desperately ill by the time we got there. A CATscan showed that his brain was squashed into a fifth of his skull and the rest of the skull was filled with blood. The surgeon gave him a 30 per cent chance of surviving.

The week before this event, my wife, Mary, and I had been asked in our church to set up a prayer chain. I'd never imagined I'd be the first to use the prayer chain. I can remember picking up the phone and hardly being able to get the words out that my son was desperately ill and we needed prayers. When we went up to the ward for Paul to have his head shaved, there was our pastor. It was only eight o'clock on a Saturday morning, but he'd got the message through the prayer chain. He'd got on a train and gone up to London, dropping everything else. He said, "Let's pray," and two of the nurses on the ward joined us. We laid hands on Paul and prayed for him and anointed him with oil for healing. He had three very long hours in the operating theatre, and then he was not really conscious for two days. After five days he was moving normally, and the surgeon said he was doing incredibly well, considering that they'd had to remove a quarter of his skull, tie off an artery, and sew the skull back again. But he would have to take anti-convulsant drugs for a year.

A week after the operation, Paul was home, in church, all bandaged up, and we gave our testimony to God's love. We just shared what God had done. On Sunday we realized that the hospital had forgotten to give Paul his anticonvulsant medicine. He's now thirteen and at grammar school. He's completely well and he's never had any medicine. You can explain it medically: he was one of the 30 per cent of cases that do wonderfully well. But it was the power of prayer and the skill of medicine combined that brought a wonderful outcome for us.

And at Burrswood, we see that every day. It's medicine and prayer coming together to change lives in the name of Jesus.

When a doctor tells a patient that he or she has three months to live, is that a kind of curse that can actually cause the patient to die in three months?

There's a part of overcoming illness that is not yet scientifically understood. To the extent that we all need hope, a prognosis that predicts a time limit to a life may act like a curse. Undoubtedly, if we go into depression, our ability to fight off illness is diminished. If we have hope and determination, our antibodies are higher, and that is well proven. False optimism is unhelpful, yet we need to be aware of hope as being important for all of us. I think it's important for people to be given the reality of their prognosis, but sometimes doctors get it wrong or treatments are unexpectedly helpful — or God intervenes.

I was talking to a man last night who, just six weeks ago, having been completely well, was told that he had only a few months to live. He said he had come seeking either a miracle of entering God's presence in heaven or a miracle of being cured. He said he valued being told he had only a few months to live because, with a young family, he needed to get his house in order. Also, although the prognosis filled him first with a sense of despair, he then felt determination to prove the doctor wrong. For him it wasn't a sentence because he had the inner resources and the faith to overcome it. But some people who are more melancholic or who haven't a faith are more likely to curl up and give up. We have all seen elderly couples who are very close. The wife dies suddenly and the husband goes into deep despair and gives up as if he had put that curse on himself.

I believe that we have a responsibility to one another and that we can influence the course of things. The dying can be very aware of when they're going to die, and those around the one who is dying can influence the moment of death. Sometimes people let go more readily when the one they love most has left the room. The family have given that person a gift by releasing them to die because they were ready to go. That, too, is a form of healing.

GOD NEVER IGNORES PRAYERS FOR HEALING

MICHAEL FULLJAMES, *a priest, is the senior chaplain at Burrswood.*

Why does God seem to ignore some people's suffering?

I don't think God ignores suffering, but ultimately it's a mystery why one person is cured and another is not. Why is there suffering in the world at all? Why did Jesus have to suffer and die? As Christians, we hold very clearly that Jesus took the suffering and used it to make something good — and he showed this by rising from death. For us, this is a very subtle message that invites us to respond by saying, "We'll meet this head on. We'll take the suffering, we'll live with it, we'll use it, we'll change it, we'll make something good out of it." When we join ourselves to Christ's work in that way, God triumphs over all suffering.

I think one of our tasks here is to actually show people the nature of suffering. Sometimes we suffer because we feel helpless in our humanity. That's very salutary because it makes us realize that our medical skills and counselling skills have limits:

we really do have to depend on God. If we feel that we are depending more on our Lord Jesus Christ than on our own skills or words, then we're likely to be on the right track.

Conflict rarely occurs here at Burrswood between the scientifically trained medical people and those who believe in the power of prayer to heal. We work together as a team of people, committed to the understanding that Christ's healing power works. But sometimes we feel as though we're being undermined, as though there's some enemy trying to divide us or deceive us, and we pray against that. When God's work is being done, the powers of darkness don't like it. We have to be on our guard to keep in the right direction, God's direction. To claim this territory for Christ, we go through the whole house every year, praying in every room.

We do see a lot of people at Burrswood who have been deeply harmed by others. They may be victims of abuse; physical, sexual, emotional, spiritual. With deep counselling we help them to address what has happened to themselves, to admit that even loved ones may have abused them in some way. When they can recognize their resentment, sometimes we're able to help them to release it and to work towards the possibility of forgiveness. Forgiveness is more a decision than a feeling, a decision to treat people as though you loved them. With sufferers we can pray Jesus Christ into a time past, so that they realize that he was there with them, weeping as they wept. In these ways, people have been released from the things that were holding them in sickness or a sick way of life. Often we see light come back into dark lives. We see evidence of God working through people, so that those hurts that have been perpetrated by others, wittingly or unwittingly, can actually be healed.

There is some evidence that emotional hurts can manifest physically. And it can work the other way; physical sickness can affect your mood. Other hospitals in Britain are under enormous pressure to feed the patient through quickly because there's a queue out there waiting. Here at Burrswood, we take time to look at every aspect of people and then minister to them.

When I lay hands on someone for healing, I feel great empathy and sympathy for them. The faith part of me is praying to God: "Be with this person. Relieve this person of those things that are causing her or him to experience pains, fears, hurts, sicknesses, sorrow. Release them, set them free, and refresh them, so that with courage and confidence they can live the way that You want them to live and be more and more the person You want him or her to be." I think that's what healing's about; becoming the person God wants us to be, so that we can fulfil the purpose for which we're created.

WHEN YOU PRAY FOR HEALING, NOTHING NEVER HAPPENS

WENDY DIMMOCK'S *varied nursing career began in England, and after a spell in Africa, continues in Canada. A visit to Burrswood as a member of the team approved by the Bishop of Toronto has inspired her to work towards the establishment of a similar centre in Toronto while continuing to build on the healing ministry in her own church.*

When did you begin to feel that spirituality was part of the process of healing?

For a long time I have known that it isn't just the body that needs to be healed, but the whole person. At the very beginning of my nursing career the spiritual aspect was not there, although I had grown up in a Christian family and had gone to church. I call to mind an incident when I was a young nurse, about twenty years old. A little boy, six years old, was dying of leukemia. I remember the strength that little boy gave to his family and to the nurses. At the end I remember him saying to his parents, "Don't worry, I'll be all right. I hear bells ringing and I see the angels coming to take me to heaven." At that point he slipped away. I suppose this was not conscious spirituality on his part, but it was very powerful and I'll never forget it. After I began nursing in Canada, I did a year's training in wellness because it was becoming evident to me that there was more to it than healing the body.

Christian healing doesn't necessarily mean physical cure. It's about preparing us for that pilgrimage to the kingdom of God, where we will be whole in body, mind, and spirit. I think we have to pray expectantly because we clearly want the person to be physically healed, but we also have to move aside and make room for God's will. It's God who is the healer.

Why are some people cured and not others?

That's a hard question. When I went to Burrswood, the Christian healing centre in England, I saw how they work with the mystery of suffering and healing. One of the doctors there once said to me that Christian healing is the strength to live, the strength to suffer, and the strength to die. It is not only about physical cure and getting better and not hurting. It's about living when there is pain and suffering. Some people are physically cured; others may be emotionally cured but not physically cured; others may be spiritually cured but not physically cured.

I experienced a very profound emotional healing at Burrswood. Just before leaving to go there, I saw a TV program in which Sir Harry Secombe visited Burrswood. In one scene, beside a beautiful lily pond in the grounds, a choir of little boys sang a very beautiful Celtic benediction. The camera zoomed in on a cherubic boy as he sang. It so happens that this benediction was inscribed on my mother's grave. The words are, "Deep peace of the Running Wave to you, deep peace of the Flowing Air to you, deep peace of the Quiet Earth to you, deep peace of the Shining Stars to you, deep peace of the Son of Peace to you." My relationship with my mother had not been peaceful. That TV show held a message for me.

So when I went to Burrswood, I found the lily pond and I sat there many days and prayed often. I prayed by the pond and I prayed in the church to find that peace. And I found it. I had wrestled with feelings of guilt and I was looking for forgiveness and I found it. Since that experience, I don't have those feelings of remorse and guilt and sadness about my mother. That was for me an experience of emotional healing. I think it was God's will. I mean, why was I selected to go to Burrswood and why did that video come on the week before I was to go and why did it have that blessing? Perhaps God wanted to help me understand that healing is all-encompassing. Now, in my work as a nurse, I think about God's love and healing power and the power of prayer in healing. I think of how at Burrswood they look at every person with love and understanding and see Jesus in each one of them.

Please describe the lay anointing in which you are involved.

Anointing with oil for healing is an outward and a visible sign of the healing grace of Christ. I have been trained as a lay anointer. It was an intensive training program. I had to be approved, upheld, and supported in that training by the parish priest and the congregation. We learned about the history of anointing in Old Testament times and about how the apostles anointed and healed people in New Testament times. Now, along with about sixty other people, ordinary lay parishioners, I have been licensed by the bishop to anoint people at healing services. The hope is that our churches will be seen as places of hope and healing and wholeness.

At our healing service, time is limited for each person, so we ask only for the person's name, or, if they're coming for healing for someone else, we ask for that person's name. If they want, they may explain a little about their need. Then we pray for their wholeness in body, mind, and spirit, and pray that they will feel the healing presence and love of Christ and be healed according to his will. We are merely the channels; Christ is the healer.

I think what happens is this: when you pray with a person for healing, you try to feel that person's need, to be at one with that person and with Christ at the same time, to allow Christ's healing power to flow through you and into that person. You envisage holding Christ, that person, and you together in the crucible of your heart. Then, in some way, the healing power flows through you and into the other person.

We know that God works in very mysterious ways. He doesn't always do what we pray for. But Miriam Dobell, the lady who was healed at Burrswood and continued a healing ministry here in Toronto, always said, "When you pray for healing, nothing never happens."

A HEALING CENTRE MINISTERS TO BODY, MIND, AND SPIRIT

TREVOR DENNY *is the incumbent of St. Peter's Anglican Church in Scarborough, Ontario, and spokesperson for the Diocese of Toronto's Healing Centre Committee.*

≈≈≈

How do you think God's healing power is actually made present through prayer?

Healing covers a vast spectrum of things. People caring, praying, supporting — all contribute to healing. I believe that God is not confined to one method of healing.

When a person prays to be healed, the prayer is a means by which they focus their thinking. They may use a picture of Jesus or an icon as a focus to envisage God's presence and the receiving of his power and strength. In times of silent prayer, people may feel his presence and this energizes them. They learn to focus, to meditate, to reflect, to relax in God's spirit.

When you pray for a sick person or lay hands on them, some kind of energy passes from the person who's laying on the hands to the person who's being healed. I believe as a Christian that, when I pray that the Holy Spirit may touch this person through me, I'm just a vehicle of this energy that's being directed in love.

Prayer is the transmission of love and concern for people. When I pray for someone's healing, I pray for God's best for that person. Sometimes when I see a person suffering, something inside me says, "Let this person go and be at rest," and sometimes the miracle of healing is the person's death. Always in prayer there is the aspect of being released in peace. Healing is for the spirit and the mind as well as the body.

Every church should be a healing centre where people come to have peace, relaxation, and support groups, and where prayers are made for healing. It's a very good thing for healing to be a sacramental part of worship, connected closely with the Holy Communion, so that people can recognize the sacramental nature of healing. Evangelism is an important part of healing because evangelism is bringing people to salvation. The word salvation means wholness, health, and holiness.

Priests are called in their ordination vows to preach, teach, and heal. Many priests already practise a ministry of healing without any fanfare; it's a natural part of their ministry. They visit in hospitals, place a hand on a patient's head or hold their hand, or anoint them with the oil of healing.

But the healing ministry is not just going into a hospital and putting your hand on a sick person's head. It includes the great crowd of unseen witnesses who are praying, people who are caring and offering practical support, counselling groups, and groups of people in churches who pray with a sick person.

Can you tell us something about your efforts to found a healing centre here in Canada?

W e're looking for a place, preferably in the country, that would suggest peace to people. It should be a beautiful place, perhaps with prayer gardens. It might be part hospital, part retreat house, part conference centre. It would provide extensive counselling — caring people who will listen. We want to create a centre that ministers to body, mind, and spirit as Burrswood in England does. Although there are more healing centres in England than in Canada, many with a special focus on addiction, psychiatric problems, or certain kinds of medical conditions, we have the Manitoba Wellness Centre in Winnipeg, where they concentrate on addictions. The essential feature of a healing centre is that it's a place set aside where people can rest and feel God's presence through the care they receive.

Right now, we're gathering support. Doctors see the value of it, and many are very interested. They know that many patients don't need medications but could be helped through counselling. Right now, with the cutbacks in the health service, nurses and doctors are very frustrated, so they like the idea of a place that is really supportive of patients. Obviously, a big question is how to finance it, and we're getting people involved in saving, donating, and fundraising. We need support of all kinds, including money, but we also need prayers. What matters most is the vision of what it might be.

People Are Trained To Be Spiritual Healers

Bishop Morris Maddocks *was the Advisor for the Ministry of Health and Healing to the Anglican Archbishops of Canterbury and York. He was also Director of the Acorn Christian Healing Trust. His initiatives include training Acorn staff at Burrswood "to bridge the gap between spirituality and medicine."*

What are the principles on which a Christian healing ministry can be built?

We rightly place our emphasis on Jesus' teaching and life, including his death and resurrection, but we need to regain an understanding of his healing ministry. Time and again in the gospels, we hear that Jesus taught and healed — the two have to go together. That, I think, is the message of the New Testament. The apostles were very obedient to their Lord's example; they both taught and healed.

Jesus healed people at three levels. All good doctors work at the first two. First, they consider the symptoms that the patient is presenting — those of a rotten cold, for instance. Second, they then ask themselves what lies beneath the symptoms. Is the patient having trouble at work or at home, for instance? Our Lord adds a third level: care for spiritual needs. When he cured the woman who had a hemorrhage, he made sure that he found out who she was and discovered her spiritual need. By the way, St. Luke, in whose gospel that story appears, was a doctor, called by St. Paul "the beloved physician." His gospel contains many stories of healing, often with exact medical terminology.

Healing is a journey to total wholeness. It may involve the cure of a disease; it may mean spiritual advance. Probably it will mean both as we advance to the fullness of the stature of Christ. God's will is for our wholeness. We can think of DNA as a program for health that God has put into our bodies, and our immune system is a wonderful preventive of sickness.

The old idea, perpetuated in part by the *Book of Common Prayer*, that sickness is a punishment given by God, needs re-examination, and I think we've got beyond it. God never wishes ill to anyone. Sometimes a sickness can be a wake-up call, because when people are afflicted with a terrible disease and do not know where to turn, they have been helped to turn to God and to faith in Jesus Christ. However, aging is a reality and the body must eventually die. That makes it all the more important to consider the spiritual aspects of healing. Four relationships are vital to good health: our relationship with God, with the creation, with our neighbours, and with ourselves.

How does prayer assist healing?

I t's very important. While working in the Diocese of York, I helped start fellowships of healing prayer, and they undergirded all the healing work we did. Twenty-five years later, these groups still regularly meet. I've felt them praying when I've been hundreds of miles away.

Prayer is being with God. Although it takes concentration to be with God and not to be carried away by the distractions that float into our mind, prayer doesn't necessarily need a lot of practice. Anyone can say, "Lord, I believe. Help my unbelief." The immediate, spontaneous prayer of a stricken child is bound to be effective. Being with God doesn't even require words; in fact, sometimes words get in the way as, for example, when we give God a shopping list of things we want. Prayer is two-way communication in which we must listen to God just as we expect God to listen to us.

Sometimes it seems that God is not listening to us or is answering with a resounding No! But when he closes one door, he usually opens another, and we have to be ready to continue our journey to wholeness in the way that God directs.

How can those interested in spiritual healing work together with medical doctors?

The Christian healer must bring compassion and caring to the sufferer. A doctor may have thirty or forty patients in the waiting room, and there isn't time to sit with each patient for an hour and discover what his or her deep needs are. Yet what people desperately need is someone who will listen to them. Doctors need support from people who know something about spiritual healing. For example, a lot of people carry an immense burden of guilt. Our Lord says to them, "Come to me, you who are heavily burdened, and I will refresh you." By listening to people, we can help them to unpack these burdens, and we can assure them of our Lord's resurrection gift of peace. Thanks to pioneers like Dr. Herbert Benson, there is a growing awareness among doctors of the spiritual dimension in healing and of the need for listening. We haven't been listening to people as we should, but more and more people are realizing that, when sick people are listened to, they feel released and helped.

When I was appointed the advisor on healing to the Archbishops of Canterbury and York, together with my wife, Anne, I began the Acorn Christian Healing Trust, which has initiated many healing ministries. It was our plan to train an apostolate of Christians dedicated to healing, who would work in teams of two, of which one would be medically trained. We hoped in this way to bridge the gap between spirituality and medicine. Over a period of four years we trained 160 people at Burrswood, including doctors, nurses, and clergy, and they have gone on to take wonderful initiatives. A doctor and a vicar set up a house of healing in a very deprived area of Gateshead in Newcastle-upon-Tyne. There is a home for the mentally handicapped and sick on the Isle of Wight. Since then, we've initiated a program of bishops' advisors in the Church of England and trained the people to be advisors. We've held festivals of healing in the cathedrals, which have brought the tiny groups of people interceding for healing, say, in a small village, together with others. They have been strengthened by discovering that hundreds of people are involved in this work.

I think that in the future we must turn our attention to the healing of nations. It's very impressive that at this moment a lot of healing is taking place in Northern Ireland. We must also work for healing among ethnic groups. All these efforts need the support of prayer.

A FAMILY AND A PARISH PRAYER GROUP ASSIST HEALING

BOB PRIESTMAN *is a retired businessman. For twenty years he has been a lay reader and a member of his parish healing committee, which is chaired by Wendy Dimmock.*

How have you become convinced that prayer has a role in healing?

Thirty-five years ago I contracted a serious illness and I was in the hospital with such excruciating pain that I wanted to die. Finally after three weeks I said, "God, I can't handle this any longer; just do whatever you want with me. I'm yours." I'm not saying that that's the reason I got better, but I did get better. During the nine months of recovery that followed, the big question I kept asking and praying about was: why had I been healed? I got an answer as clear as if the fellow in the next bed had said it aloud to me: "I've got things for you to do." That didn't mean very much at the time, but after I got back on my feet, I became a counsellor to young people and that was the most exhilarating experience of my life.

I'll tell you another story. I had cornea transplant operations on both eyes, and afterwards I couldn't read, couldn't drive. No lenses could be found that worked. Then, at the cottage at Thanksgiving, my kids were discussing their churches. My wife reminded them to pray for my eyes. All seven of them then stood around me in a circle, put their hands on my shoulders and my head, and prayed. Two days later when I went to the doctor, he said, "I'm going to try something on you." Then he put a special contact lens in my eye and I could see perfectly! My eyes hadn't healed, but my sight had been given back. Sometimes when we pray, we don't recognize the healing that follows.

Here's another story. My wife had a heart attack at the cottage while she was out picking berries. We got her to the hospital quickly and she was recovering nicely. But then she started having angina problems, and they decided to operate. They replaced six veins, which is the maximum, but afterwards she was doing so well that the doctor told me to go and have dinner and come back later. When I returned, she was on every kind of life support you can think of. Everything had gone wrong. For fifteen days she didn't move a muscle. We have a prayer chain at our church and she was put on the prayer chain, and she was also prayed for in our family's churches in Oakville and Bracebridge, Ontario, and at a cousin's church in England. Some friends who were touring China heard about it and were praying, too. She was receiving prayers from all the world over, and she got better.

Each day I went to visit her in hospital. One cold day in winter when it was still dark in the early morning and there was very little traffic, I was walking to the hospital along the sidewalk covered with ice and snow. When I stopped at a stop light, I thought I heard someone speaking behind me, but there was nobody there. But the voice kept saying, "Don't worry. I'm taking care of her."

I don't believe a loving God allows pain and suffering. We don't know why these things happen; that's God's business. Our business is to react the way God wants us to react to these events. God is perfection and can tolerate no imperfection. Christ took all our imperfections on himself and died and was judged absolutely guiltless and took his place beside the Father. Because he did this for us, if we trust in him, we'll have the same result.

HEALING BRINGS ABOUT A CHANGE IN LIFE AND RELATIONSHIPS

DEREK WADDELL, *a Toronto hairdresser, was diagnosed as HIV positive. He describes his experience of healing with help from prayer.*

Can you describe how healing has come about in your life?

I was working, I was partying — basically living life the way I thought everybody would like me to lead it. I didn't respect my life.

When I was diagnosed the doctor told me I had three years to live. I was a babbling mess. I could hardly even pick up the phone to tell people. And I was scared that I was going to be a burden to all those people that loved me. I've always been independent. My parents divorced when I was thirteen. I was working when I was fifteen. I had my own apartment when I was sixteen. I think it's really hard for people to ask for help. It's something I've learned recently; that asking for help is okay.

Now, looking back, it's weird, but I'm really glad I was diagnosed positive because I've bettered my life and I've improved my relationships with everybody, including myself. One of the very important things for me to do was to clean up my relationships. There were people I didn't even talk to — we'd fallen out or they'd aggravated me because they weren't doing things my way.

When I found out I was HIV positive, it was as if I had to come out of the closet again with my family. They had dealt with the fact that I'm gay, but now I was gay and I was going to die. I dreaded having that deep conversation with my family, but when I did, they came forward and asked, "What do you need?" And they said, "We don't love you any less, and we're here for you." So, I got a better relationship with my family, too.

Then I found out that people I'd known for twenty years, who weren't religious, were praying for me. There seems to be a stigma against talking about praying. People are actually doing it, but they won't admit it — like closet prayers.

About four years ago, a friend of mine invited me to go to the Metropolitan Community Church. I didn't want to go because church didn't mean anything much when I was a kid, but this church is so non-judgemental, so loving, so caring that it was easy to go. And then it was easy to say to myself after that: I can go home and pray now. I always believed in God and I still do. But what God looked like to me then and what God looks like now is totally different. If I needed to pass an exam or to get my driver's licence, I'd think, "Please, God, get me through this." And it always worked. I think I got lost in coming out of the closet and in dealing with my homosexuality.

But I knew I was gay and I knew I had to come to that life and make a deal with it, even if it was not approved of by my family or by the church.

Then this friend at the church said, "I can ask a bunch of people to pray for you." I said, "If you want to do that, that's cool." He said, "Absolutely, not a problem. Just remember all those things we learned about healing and taking care of yourself and meditation." These people started to support me and brought so much love back to me. I don't go to church every Sunday, but I know all that energy is out there, and it really makes a difference.

And when I started to feel better, I felt my life had been given back to me, with forty-seven years of wisdom. Now I want to do the best I can with it. I think I've been a healer through hairdressing. People are needy, and many clients just sit in the chair and all of a sudden they're crying. So I've done a lot of healing that way. It's as if you've got this wisdom and you take it out and share it to help someone.

I feel I'm sustained now by the prayers of others. When all I had was the shell of a body with the virus running through it and I was going to die soon, that was the darkest spot. I just wanted to die. But I accepted the dark place. I needed to go there to mess around in the mud and the mire. I needed to know what it was about. And then I needed to get out of there. Negativity is one of the easiest things to come by. You grab it from every person you know, and it grows fast. Positive stuff is hard to come by. It's like diamonds. When those little shiny diamonds came by, I missed them. Now everything has changed.

I pray every night. I thank God for just the day. I can't say that if I get really sick, I'm going to get down on my knees and say, "Please haul me out of this." But I give thanks for my joys

— flowers, or hearing that somebody did something really good, or that they got a job.

My eldest nephew was diagnosed with lung cancer at thirty-five and I really wish I could go and pray with him. He's totally not the kind of person who's going to pray. If anything, he's going to buy stronger cigarettes and drink twice as many beers. He never really had a girlfriend, but when he was going through some chemotherapy a little while ago, he met a lovely lady and through all this pain, love has come in. He won't die without having felt love. It's as if God has taken something away and given something bigger in return. I can give thanks for something like that.

PALLIATIVE CARE IS HEALING THE DYING

BEVERLY SPRING *is a palliative care physician who works at a major hospital in Vancouver. She is also a hospice physician for those who choose to die at home.*

How can you speak of healing when you know the patient is terminally ill and will soon die?

Medical training teaches us to believe that we can fix whatever the problem is, and our whole culture supports that model of doing and fixing. In palliative care, you're confronted with the fundamental fact that you can't fix the problem. People often come to us after they have been told that nothing more can be done for them, and they have only a short time to live. Being told this leaves the terminally ill patient feeling abandoned, and the medical practitioners feeling powerless. We all need to surrender to the mystery of ultimately not being able to control things.

Of course, there is much we can do to make patients comfortable and to ensure a certain quality of life for as long as they live. For example, I do a lot of teaching about pain and symptom management.

But there is more to it than that. What I do is certainly not religious, and to call it spiritual makes it sound esoteric. When I let go of my role as a doctor and meet a patient as a human being, the patient can let go of the role of patient, and a meeting occurs in a place that is beyond our roles and beyond our personalities, and beyond our separateness. It is very profound, and it is this connection of the heart that is truly healing for both the giver and the receiver of care.

Recently I cared for a young woman for three months, managing her analgesics, her shortness of breath, and her bowel problems. But I also came to love her and I felt that she loved me. I was on an airplane when she died, so I missed the moment of her death. But at the moment when she died, I felt a tightening in my chest and started to cry. It wasn't until later when I phoned that I learned she had died. This relationship that developed as she was confronting the deepest issues of her life was so enriching that the rest of life pales beside it.

I remember a very successful young lawyer who had done all the right things to be healthy — ate the right foods, rode his bike to work — but he got a cancer that progressed very rapidly. He was very angry, and every time I saw him he would play the same angry story over and over again. He was so angry that he didn't want to see his teenaged kids or have much to do with his wife. I was afraid he would never let go and would die angry. I just listened to him without interrupting, trying to feel open-heartedness towards him, trying to feel his pain and his sadness. Then one day he said he had woken up and started to priorize all the things he had to do, and then suddenly asked himself, "What really needs doing? — Nothing! Who really needs to do it? — Nobody!" He couldn't find the words to describe what happened next, but then he said, "I've never felt such peacefulness before." His anger vanished, and soon he was telling everyone how much he loved them.

In cases like these, my role is to be a kind of catalyst whom people can depend on to provide consistent love and support. Sometimes I just sit with them without saying a word. Although I don't actually pray for them, in a way I try to beam some energy towards them, and I send them loving thoughts that encourage them to be courageous and let them know that it is okay for them to let go. But the healing that results comes from within themselves. There's a big mystery here; the experience of dying brings about a transformative process in the person, which is utterly beautiful.

Part 4

THE PERSPECTIVE
OF OTHER FAITHS

A JEWISH PERSPECTIVE

RABBI RONALD WEISS *is Director of Chaplaincy services for the Toronto Jewish community. He is also the chaplain for the Jewish Hospice Program.*

Is prayer for healing part of the Jewish tradition?

Prayer has always been a very basic part of the communication between man and God. We believe that, by opening the heart, all Jewish people have immediate access to the Almighty, a personal relationship with God. The medium of communication is prayer. There are three different aspects of prayer. Thanksgiving — *ho-da-ah* — is required to thank God for the blessings that we receive. Praise — *shevach* — is required to praise God for having given us the world as it is. Requests —*bakashoat* — are petitions in which we ask God for things that we feel we need. People have always felt a tremendous gratitude towards God and a need to ask for what they feel is lacking in their lives.

Learning to master the skill of prayer is a life-long endeavour. Jewish people have always focused on the study of religious texts. It is the way we communicate with God and the way God communicates with us. By studying the tradition we find the way that God wants us to live. There is dialogue between, on the one hand, tradition speaking to us and, on the other, prayer and study as our means of articulating what is within us and offering our souls back to God. By this dialogue, we further our spiritual growth and develop our relationship with the Almighty.

As soon as our children begin to speak, we teach them how to pray, beginning with certain prayers at certain times of the day. As the children grow, they continue with religious training appropriate to the different stages in their lives. Prayer becomes a part of them.

There is an aspect of prayer that is fixed routine, but there is also an aspect of prayer that is spontaneous, reflecting the specific circumstances of the individual who is praying. We use fixed prayers three times a day — morning, afternoon, and evening — whose established text provides a sense of cohesion among Jews. Around the world, in Canada or Israel or Russia, people are saying the same words at the same time of the day. Therefore, despite being of different nationalities, they are speaking the same language culturally, religiously, spiritually. But there are also places in the prayers where the individual petitioners can add what is appropriate for them. Prayer fosters a sense of belonging to community and clearly identifies your role in society. It gives you a focus and a reference point. It provides you with the companionship of people and fosters your relationship with the Almighty. For Jews, there is no intermediary between themselves and God. Prayer is a direct communication.

There is no scientific way of measuring the effectiveness of prayer, but you don't have to convince those who use prayer of its power. They see it and understand it. Jews believe that there is always a response to prayer, although it may not always be the response we want to hear. God doesn't need our prayers. The purpose of prayer is for the individual to feel closer to God. It's not so much the answer that matters, but the feeling that God is listening that is of critical importance. People can deal with almost any tragedy, almost any crisis, if they feel that they have not been abandoned by the Almighty, irrespective of what his answer is to a particular request. Feeling that God cares about you can give you tremendous spiritual strength, and with spiritual strength you can overcome virtually any physical circumstance.

There's an old story about a brother and sister who were playing. The little boy was teasing his sister, and she dropped the doll she was playing with. The doll broke. The little boy asked teasingly, "You love that doll. How are you going to get it fixed?" "I'm going to pray to God," she said. She prayed and time passed. "Is your doll fixed?" the boy asked. "Did God listen to you?" And the girl replied, "God answered me. God said No." We only want to accept the answers from God that we're looking for, but the wisdom of the little girl in the story was in her recognizing that No was the response appropriate to her situation. After time has passed and when circumstances are different, the girl will be able to see the situation of her broken doll from a different perspective and understand things differently.

Judaism has always had specific prayers for those who are ill. There's a prayer called the *Misha Barach* in which we invoke God's blessing on those who are ill. The entire congregation assembled lends the weight of their prayers to the request for the well-being of these individuals. In our individual private prayers, there is a section where you can add to the names of the sick. We believe that all members of the community are intimately responsible for each other and are required to assist by giving physical or financial support and by praying for each other. Jewish religious law legislates prayer on behalf of those who are ill.

As a chaplain, do you see yourself as a healer?

Of course. A chaplain tries to be a facilitator of healing, but he has to be careful of the boundaries set by the people he's dealing with. Sometimes I go in as a rabbi, sometimes I go in as a chaplain, sometimes I go in as a friend. Sometimes I get thrown out of a hospital room by a patient. Sometimes patients look to me for guidance and direction in understanding what Judaism says about their particular situation. Sometimes they're angry at God; "How could God do this to me?" I get a feel for people's needs by talking to them. Often they'll tell me flat out what it is they want or there's enough body language to tell me.

Often I deal not only with the patients, but also with their families. In the Jewish community the patient and the family are viewed almost as a unit, and you care for the unit. For example, a patient with a terminal illness may have accepted that he or she is dying, but the family hasn't. How do you try to reconcile the fact that the patient is trying to say goodbye and the family doesn't want to hear it? The reverse could also be true; the family knows the patient is dying and the patient is hoping for a cure. They are adversaries only because they love each other.

Healing is not always providing a cure. Healing is providing a way of understanding and dealing with the reality of your situation. Terminally ill people don't always expect to be cured of their illness, but we can provide a measure of healing simply by refocusing their expectations. We don't take away their hope, but if we can help them to transform hope for a longer life into hope for a meaningful life, however long God sees fit to allow life to continue, we have given a measure of healing.

We deal primarily with the individual's spirituality or religious outlook — the relationship the individual has or could develop with God, using the Jewish community and traditions as a resource to draw upon for comfort and encouragement. I belong to a group of Jewish professionals and lay people who are trying to respond to the need for healing, recognizing that organized Jewish religious expression doesn't satisfy everyone. Many people in our community who are ill and in need of healing don't feel comfortable in a synogogue or with the organized prayers, but they're very attuned to certain cultural aspects of being Jewish. So our healing project tries to provide an alternative that recognizes Jewish values, Jewish beliefs, and Jewish traditions, but doesn't bring the package of ritual or organization that puts some people off. We are having some success.

We don't insist on prayer, but we use meditation. A lot of prayer is meditation, but if you call it meditation instead of prayer, sometimes it's more palatable for those who are more secular in their orientation. We use breathing exercises to help patients align their inner sense of being with the reality of their lives. This is a spiritual activity.

I think the medical world is beginning to recognize that you can't care for someone physically and expect them to get better if their spiritual needs are not also recognized and met. Hospitals have chaplains because, when patients' treatment recognizes and responds to their spirituality, they feel more comfortable and their convalescence may be shorter. Sometimes people don't know what their spiritual needs are, and a chaplain can help identify them. Sometimes people are frightened, and the religious tradition can provide a grounding on which they find strength or comfort.

Healing is different for each person. One of the good things about a spiritual approach to healing is that it is not locked into certain formulae. It considers not only physical needs, but also mental and spiritual orientation.

AN ISLAMIC PERSPECTIVE

HAROON SALAMAT *is a professional engineer. He is also Chairman of the Toronto and Region Islamic Congregation and Chairman of Al Shura, the Muslim Consultative Council of the Greater Toronto area.*

Could we begin with some comments on the significance of prayer in Islamic life?

The significance of prayer is communication with God. It is remembering God in everything that you do and attributing whatever you have to him. This communication goes on continuously in your life. When you see a Muslim you will not necessarily just say, "Good morning"; you will say, "May the peace of God be with you." So you remember God. If someone says, "It's a beautiful day," you will say, "Glory be to God." If someone asks after your child and the child is healthy, you will say, "He is well. Praise be to God." You remember God in everything that you do and say. This remembrance is continued in the prescribed prayers, five times a day, called the *Salat*. It is said that noon prayer, for example, is an opportunity to ask for forgiveness for any mistakes that you have made between the morning prayer and noon time. Similarly, mid-afternoon prayer is another opportunity to erase any mistakes that you might have made between noon and mid-afternoon and so forth. Prayer is a continuing atonement for sins, communication with God, and a thanking of God for whatever God has given you.

In Islam there are several types of prayers. The prayers I have just mentioned, made regularly five times a day, are devotional prayers in the sense that you don't ad lib; you do exactly what the prayer requires you to do. These prayers are only for God. You do not ask for anything for yourself during a devotional prayer. However, during a supplication, you can ask for anything you want. Generally when you're finished the formal part of your prayer, you raise your hands and ask for a better job, more money, a good family, to forgive your parents — whatever you wish; this kind of prayer is open-ended.

Is there a recognized connection between prayer and healing in Islam?

The Koran says, "In this book is guidance and cure." It literally means that whatever ails you can be cured by reading the Koran and meditating on it. So although the mosque does not advertise itself as a place of healing, healing comes from doing all the forms of worship: praying, giving charity to the poor, fasting, making the *haj* (the pilgrimage to Mecca once in your lifetime). These are all part of the healing process. Each day when you pray those five daily prayers, you repeat, "You alone we worship and you alone we ask for help." The only being to whom you go for assistance is God. This doesn't mean that you do not go to your doctor, but when the doctor heals, it is God healing through the doctor and using his techniques.

At the end of the prescribed prayers, as I have said, while you sit and contemplate God, there is an opportunity to ask for healing. Sometimes in the mosque the leader of the prayer, the *imam*, will ask everyone to raise their hands and make a *dowa* for someone who is ill. Then we all join in reciting some familiar verses from the Koran. To phrase this asking for help, we go back to the Hadith, which are the sayings and practices of the Prophet, and we find there many instances where the Prophet asked for assistance for people who were ill, people who were travelling, people who were in distress. But the healing comes from God only, and it's up to God to decide whether he will heal a person or not. We accept whatever the decision is.

In Islam, we believe first and foremost that God is in command and He knows everything that is happening and will happen. God knows whether this person will die or not die. We do not know. When we ask for healing for an individual, we're asking God to assist this person to get better, but we are prepared to accept whatever decision God makes. Even if the person dies, we say, "Praise be to God, it is His will." A Muslim believes that what is going to happen will happen and we have no control over it. All we can do is to ask God that whatever happens is not going to be so burdensome that we cannot bear it. We ask that the pain be acceptable to us, even easy for us, so that we are not overwhelmed by this disaster; and we ask for strength to carry on and for an unwavering faith. When a *dowa* is accepted and the person recovers miraculously, we know that the healing has come from God.

Sometimes, I'm sure, individuals will ask, "Why has this bad thing happened to me?" But ultimately, if you are a believer, you will accept it and get on with life. Muslims know that there is an after-life and the after-life is better than this life, according to the Koran. Life on earth is a test, and if we pass this test, we will achieve paradise, which is a period of bliss, calm, serenity, tranquillity, and peace. No matter who we are, we are going to die, whether at twenty-one years of age or ninety-one. Now, it's very difficult when a young person dies, but as a person gets older, we expect that he will die. We hope the death will not be painful and that the person will die fulfilled and appreciated by those around him. There must be acceptance of this passing on. The people who are distraught when a loved one dies are usually consoled by those around them, told that they must accept what comes because, obviously, no one can do anything about it anyway. Those left behind must continue with life.

Almost every day, especially in chronic care wards of hospitals with cancer patients who are terminally ill, it is found that those who have faith tend to suffer less and accept what is happening to them more. When they die, they go peacefully into the night, so to speak. Non-believers seem to have a more difficult time with illnesses, especially terminal illnesses. I think this is explained by the fact that in Islam we accept whatever comes from God because He has a master plan. We fit into this plan in a particular way, and when it is time for us to go, then it's part of His plan and we accept it. We accept even the suffering that comes with serious illness. Of course, we pray for relief, and I think this helps in many cases.

Many people ask us to come to the hospital and visit. We have a visitation program in which members of the community volunteer to go to the hospital and visit the sick, not only Muslims, but primarily Muslims. While there they talk to sick people besides those they have been asked to visit, and offer prayers with them. This seems to have a beneficial effect on the people.

Do you think, then, that science is only confirming what religious people have always known?

I t's good to have scientific support for the value of prayer, especially to help those people who are sceptical or who would like to see some proof. Also, many of us who are not necessarily sceptical like to have confirmation of what we believe.

Traditionally, science and religion have worked together. Many medical discoveries have been made by people who were also very learned scholars of Islam, and many Koranic verses that mention certain illnesses have been proven to be medically correct. Dr. Moore of the University of Toronto wrote a paper in which he showed that the Koran accurately describes the birth of a baby. Traditionally, the Koran has been used to obtain medically useful information. With the development of modern medicine — and many Muslim doctors have been influenced by what's happening in the West because that's where most of the technology has been developed — medical practice got away from the religion and looked for answers primarily in the sphere of science. But I think now that many doctors are trying to see if prayer combined with science will be more effective than either one alone.

Does Islam recognize a special role for healers?

W e do not have faith healers in Islam. The *imam*, the religious leader of the mosque, will know the Koran and can recite the appropriate verses. However, in Islam we also recognize individuals who, because of their piety, their prayers, and their devotion to God, achieve a certain nearness to God. A person like this is referred to as a friend of God. It is said that when these persons ask for something from God, it is usually given. And so if you know a pious person, you might ask him to pray to God to forgive you and make you well. But intercession cannot replace the individual praying for himself. You cannot ask God to forgive me if I do not ask for forgiveness myself.

I think that people who achieve nearness to God tend to be healthier. They tend to stay away from the bad habits, such as smoking and drinking, which poison the system. In other words, a true Islamic lifestyle is a healthy lifestyle.

A BUDDHIST PERSPECTIVE

ROSHI JOAN HALIFAX *is an anthropologist, a well-known author, and a Buddhist teacher at Upaya, a Buddhist study centre, which she founded in 1990 in Santa Fe, New Mexico. The centre offers courses on engaged spirituality and contemplative care of the dying through the Project on Being with Dying.*

How does healing prayer fit into the work done at a Buddhist centre like this one?

Our main objective is what is called engaged spirituality; in other words, bringing contemplative practice into helping other beings. I say "other beings" rather than "people" because a lot of our work in engaged spirituality is with the environment. Our work in healing focuses on three different groups. One is dying people. We train health care professionals from all over the world in the contemplative care of dying people; that is, in spiritually assisted dying. The second healing area in which we are working is the penitentiary system, where we are introducing contemplative practice primarily to men who are in maximum security. The third area is environmental work. We endeavour to create a context where people can understand that they are not separate from the natural world.

We're very much committed to the development of our own contemplative community here, and my two teachers, Thich Nhat Hanh and Bernie Glasman Roshi, have a very strong commitment to engaged spirituality — to social transformation.

Contemplative practice actually encompasses a wide range of activities, with prayer being one of them. Mindfulness meditation is another. Seeing our everyday lives as a way in which we can actually be mindful and compassionate is a third. But prayer is a very important part of Western culture. I was raised as a Christian in a household that prayed, and even though I've been a Buddhist since the mid-1960s, prayer is a very active part of my life and of my practice with people who are dying and their families.

Even when someone is dying, there are many ways to pray and many things to pray about. To begin with, there are prayers of gratitude. In our culture, we don't thank God enough. Gratitude is actually an expression of fundamental generosity that is one of the Perfections in Buddhism. We can open our hearts by giving thanks. What Christians call a thankful heart is very much in the spirit of Buddhist practice. But also, we can pray for a good and peaceful death. Furthermore, we can pray that suffering be transformed. We can pray to accept suffering. We can pray to forgive others or to ask others to forgive us. We can ask God to forgive us. Prayer is actually one of the strongest contributions that I know of to a contemplative or spiritual approach to dying. By prayer, a family, a community, a dying person, and caregivers can give deep, caring attention, both as a group and as individuals in silence, to the well-being not only of the dying person, but also of the community supporting the dying person. It's a way of caring that is familiar to our culture.

In Buddhism, we have ways of praying. In the southern school of Buddhism, there are *metta* practices, which we teach to caregivers. Basically, they're prayers. For example, I can say inwardly, "May I offer my care and presence unconditionally, knowing they may be met by gratitude, indifference, anger, or anguish." That prayer, which comes out of a Buddhist context, is a prayer to everything and to oneself. Another powerful prayer is, "May I be in peace and let go of my expectations."

Another form of Buddhist prayer works like this: you feel deep love for the dying person. You actually breathe in their suffering as dark, heavy, hot smoke, which you allow to break apart your sense of self-importance. Then you let the mercy of your open heart arise, so that suffering dissolves into emptiness. Then on the out-breath, you send a breath that is cool and light and healing and contains the deep aspiration that this suffering being may be transformed. That's another very strong way to pray.

Another way to pray is beyond language, in silence. You hold a deep internal, very respectful silence. You don't need words. There's a place where all being meets that is beyond language. Silence is a way to express that presence.

These are some simple examples of prayer that can be found in slightly different forms in Buddhism, Christianity, and Judaism. I think they are close to the heart of all faith traditions.

How does prayer for healing work?

B esides being a Buddhist priest, I'm also an anthropologist. Within the discipline of anthropology, I have looked at the ways in which people pray across many cultures and also at the ways they use to think ill of each other — negative prayer. I honestly don't know how prayer works, but there are very many extraordinary examples from different cultures of the beneficial effect of positive prayer and the destructive effects of negative prayer.

From a Buddhist perspective, I would say that our minds are not merely local; we're all interconnected with one another. Any good that I would wish for one being, I would wish in my heart for all beings. This seems to accord with Dr. Larry Dossey's research findings, which suggest that mind is non-local, and that one person's mind can affect other beings even from a distance. A power is imparted to prayers by their long and frequent use in cultures, and individuals can enter the power of those prayers. Many common prayers have the quality of mantra about them: the Lord's Prayer and the Hail Mary in Christian tradition, for instance, or in Buddhism, Om Mani Padma Hum — Hail to the Jewel in the Lotus — which refers to the mind of compassion and the mind of clarity in union with each other. Such prayers are part of a great continuum, and their strength is both intimate and great. For myself, I'm more committed to the unique and individual prayers that arise spontaneously from the spaciousness within the deep and open heart.

I think we are all called to stop running in our lives. Prayer is about stopping; it's not about running. Prayer is also about allowing the silence within to be present, and out of that silence comes the truth of prayer.

I think we're all healers. To heal means to make whole. I think that we are called to do three things in our lives. One is to simply be with our unknowing — to be comfortable with a mind that doesn't already know it all. The second is to bear witness to the reality of our existence, which includes both suffering and joy — to be with that reality and not feel as if we have to change it. The third is healing — making whole, both on an intimate scale and on a large scale, in whatever way is right for us. Making whole means washing the dishes, sweeping the floor, sitting with dying people, or passing legislation that helps other beings. But fundamentally, to be able "to make whole" we need a deep and open heart from which prayer naturally arises. With the prayer there also arises love, and love is non-exclusive. Love is a vision of the world as whole and completely interconnected, and love is also living in a way that makes real this sense of oneness, as best we are able.

A FIRST NATIONS PERSPECTIVE

BARBARA SHOOMSKI *is a spiritual caregiver, mainly for Aboriginal people, at the Health Sciences Centre in Winnipeg, Manitoba. People are sent there from northern Manitoba, northern Ontario, and northern Saskatchewan.*

≈≈≈

How do you bring North American Aboriginal traditions of healing into a context where Western medicine is practised?

I grew up in northern Manitoba. I was very sick when I was nine years old. My parents were trappers and were living in a camp. They took me out of school because I was really sick and took me to The Pas. The doctor said that I would die. So my parents brought me back to the camp. It was just before Easter and there was a young man there who happened to be Catholic and he told my father to go early Easter morning and get water from the river and have me drink it and wash my head with it. The whole camp prayed that I would get better, and I did. That taught me that there's more to healing than medicine. I think I was healed so that I could become a spiritual caregiver and be a living example that God heals people.

If you look at the whole person, you have to look at the spiritual, mental, and emotional parts of being. Western medicine concentrates on the body. It doesn't address the other parts. When Aboriginal people come in from up north, they're pretty stressed because they're in such a foreign environment. They're lost and scared and just need someone to talk to. In my work, I consult with doctors, but they know that Aboriginal people feel more comfortable with other Aboriginal people.

Western medicine still teaches that there's only one way, but I see a change in the younger men and women who are trying to understand. They now know that there's not only one way and that the people with no bedside manner have no place in healing. We're learning to become a healing team because, in the end, it's a community of medical people, psychologists, psychiatrists, and spiritual caregivers who bring about healing. If we work as a team, we can touch every part of the sick person's being.

How do you use prayer in healing?

I pray for the patients I see. If they're Cree — that's my language — I pray in Cree, but if they're not Aboriginal people, I pray in English. I pray from my heart. I just pray with them for whatever it is they need. I pray for whatever is best for this person, whatever God thinks this person needs in their life.

When I was a student here in the Health Sciences Centre, one day one of the volunteers came and said there was a young lady who had just had twins and they had found cancer. She said, "I think you should go and pray with her." I was standing beside her bed and I was just praying from the depths of my being, and all of a sudden I had this feeling come through me and into her. And I knew that God was there. I knew. I could feel it. It drained my body. She went home and came back for tests two weeks later — the tests were negative. So I knew at that moment God was there. That was a holy moment and you can't explain it. I think that sometimes God chooses you or me or whomever to heal through a different way, because the medical community has already given up on a person.

Why are some people healed and others not?

I ask those questions all the time. Just this past summer a little boy was brought in severely burned — 90 per cent of his body. They sent him to Boston to the burn unit — I guess it's the best in North America. His mother and grandmother went with him, but it wasn't meant to be. He died there. His dad was here in the Health Sciences Centre at the time with AIDS, so he couldn't go and talk to his son, and then two weeks after his son died, the father died. But healing came for his family. I was asked to do the eulogy for the father. And you know, I was just drained. I had to leave the city. I couldn't breathe. I had to get fresh air. The All Native Circle of the United Church was meeting out of town by the lake, so I went there, and as soon as I walked into the circle, the elders knew something had happened. The elder said, "You know, in this circle, in the evening we sit around the sacred fire and we read scripture.

We take turns, we go around the circle." So we did that. Within a few minutes of reading, we saw the eagle come around the circle and fly off into the distance over the lake. And within half a minute, a flock of geese came. The elder said to me, "You know, Barbara, that young man that died today: his family and all his relations came to meet him and we know he went to a good place." So even though, in our understanding, the healing didn't happen for his son or him, a healing had happened in the family, who had dealt with him dying of AIDS and being gay and not being well accepted in the community. You never know what the purpose of dying is. You just pray to God and thank God. Sometimes maybe some people die so others can heal.

It's a privilege, you know, to be with people in their hour of deepest need, at the moment of death. When that moment happens, it's a holy moment and you can feel the Holy Spirit there. Sure, the person dies, but we know the person is going on to a better life. And it's hard to explain it. You just have to be there and believe. I have no answers; that's just the way things go.

It's the same for everyone. I have Hindu friends, I have a friend who's a Jewish rabbi, and they have those experiences in their communities. It's one God who does these things for all people. It's not just for Christians or just for Jews, it's for everybody. But for the prayer to work I truly believe you have to be open, or at least someone in your family has to be open, to that moment. And that's all we're asked, you know. In my case, it wasn't me personally who knew that the prayer would help, but the community of believers believed that healing would happen through prayer. That's an important part of it. Sometimes in that moment before they die, a person who's always rejected whatever their initial belief system has been realizes that there truly is a power greater than all of us, and we don't understand what that is.

How do you work as a healer in the Aboriginal tradition?

My grandmother was a healer. She knew all the medicines and herbs. She was the doctor of the community and the midwife. But when a hydro dam was built in our community, we lost the tradition. The people had been isolated and their lives revolved around the church. All of a sudden, these other influences came in. Medical doctors and other people told us that the things we were doing were no good. So the gift of healing sat dormant for a generation. But then gradually the Aboriginal people started to see that the ways of the other people who came were not healthy for us. One day I went to talk to an elder — she was ninety-three years old — and she said, "We've known since the time you were a little child that healing was what you would do." I didn't know that. I needed affirmation from the community that told me, "God healed you for a reason. Now you have to go and share that with other people." I don't know the medicines the way my grandmother did. My gift is the gift of prayer and touch. I always touch because I think humans need touch, and when I touch them there's a warmth in my hands that they can feel when I'm getting ready to pray over them. Most often I just hold their hands. I believe the Holy Spirit works through this.

I think prayer and the healing touch transmit a collective energy to the sick person, but it comes from a source greater than just humans. I'll tell you a story.

I work a lot with youth, and many of them come from broken homes where there's a lot of addiction, and a lot of them end up in correctional facilities. I saw a young man whose mom had died when he was six. The people around him told him that now he was the man of the house, so he shouldn't cry. This young man went to many foster homes and ended up in a correctional facility when he was thirteen. He wanted to talk about his mom dying and he came to see me. I told him I cried when my mom died, and I was thirty-five or something.

The next time he came to visit me, he had a picture of a bear and a baby bear snuggled up together, and at the bottom it said, "Mother's love." I said, "Tell me about this picture," and he started sharing his story. It took us many visits, but finally we came to the point where he could cry for his mother. The next time he came, we did our crying together. He was now fifteen or sixteen, and he had a lot of anger. So we used to smudge together and pray. For us, smudging is getting rid of all the negative stuff. After we did smudge, he said, "Barbara, I'm going to pray for you." This particular young man has now finished high school and he's going to go to university.

My purpose is to give people hope. All I want for the kids, or for anyone, is for them to know there's something greater than they are, and whatever you understand that being to be, that being is there for you when you need help. That being might not do what you want it to do. But at least you have some understanding of God. Sometimes you might have to get angry at God because there has been so much pain in your life, such as that young man's, and you have to be rid of it. But I tell them, "God can take anything." Unfortunately a lot of people work out their anger by what they do on the street. But the most important thing is that they understand it's not just them and the world. There's always a helper.

Laughter is healing, too. One day at the Centre, I was talking to an elder from The Pas, and we were talking in Cree. We were just telling stories and we were laughing. Another lady across the hall said, "Come over here and you can laugh with us, too." So I went over. Most people who are hurt need to see someone who has that smile and laughter.

I believe that we on this continent spend a lot of money trying to figure out what it is that happens in a hospital like this, but I think it's about spirit, you know. There's a spirit greater than us that somehow feels sorry for us. If we can open ourselves to that source of healing, good things can happen.

Part 5

A HEALING PROGRAM AT A LOCAL CHURCH

HOW WE BEGAN
OUR HEALING MINISTRY

MARGERY KELLETT *is one of the founding members of the healing ministry at Christ Church Cathedral and is still active in its work. Many churches across the country have developed healing programs. The program at Christ Church Cathedral in Vancouver is an example of one that is well established and has had important effects on its church and community.*

Will you tell us something of the history of the program and how it operates today?

Our healing ministry started in the mid-70s when we were developing a pastoral care program for the parish and recognized that prayer was an essential element. The assistant priest, Virginia Briant, who was among the first women ordained to priesthood in Canada, had a special interest and experience of the ministry of prayer for healing. Inspired by Virginia, we formed a Prayer Link group of about thirty members, who pray daily for names on a list that is renewed weekly.

Soon the clergy began offering prayer for healing, with the laying on of hands and anointing, to any who wished after the Thursday noon eucharist. Of the daily eucharists, the Thursday was (and is) the best attended. At the same time it was decided to follow the service with the offering of food and fellowship. A group of parishioners, women and men, volunteered to serve a light lunch. Then a couple of years later, the clergy invited a few of those who attended the service regularly and were members of the Prayer Link to join in forming teams of one clergy person and one lay person offering the healing prayer ministry.

By 1993 the number of lay participants had grown to seven. We formed the Healing Group. We meet regularly for mutual support and education around prayer and healing. We commit ourselves to our own spiritual growth that we may be better instruments of God's love, God's healing, for those who ask our prayers.

In 1994 we decided to make the healing ministry available after the main Sunday liturgy as well. We thought it best to experiment in short time frames; so for the season of Lent and again in Advent we followed the Thursday pattern. Two people from the Healing Group were available at the conclusion of the liturgy for anyone who wished to have healing prayers. Although the ministry was well received by the congregation, numbers soon dwindled and the circumstances were not very satisfactory. The clergy were always held up and could not come to offer anointing. (The bishop has since given permission for the lay people to anoint also.) People were ready to be on their way. The church was noisy with people greeting one another and visitors wanting to see the building.

Then the following Lent, 1995, we decided to experiment with having a place for healing prayer at the same time as the communion at the main service on Sundays. On the first Sunday of Lent seven members were commissioned to the healing ministry. We undertook a program of witness and education with the congregation. Sermons focused on healing; several members spoke from personal experience; we organized evening workshops. We have never looked back.

While the Holy Communion is being administered, two members of the healing team stand by a Celtic cross on the wall and a rack of votive candles to one side of the sanctuary. A notice in the bulletin invites those wishing particular prayer for themselves or for someone else to come to the prayer station after receiving the bread and wine.

The healing team always works in pairs. The person who wishes prayer approaches, is welcomed with a gesture of open arms, and is asked their first name and what they would like prayer for. Then the members of the healing team lay hands gently on the person's shoulders (unless it is clear the person does not want to be touched), offer prayer, and anoint with oil.

We have one short prayer that serves as our template:

Spirit of the Living God,
    present with us now:
Fill you, body, mind, and spirit,
And heal you of all that harms you,
    In Christ's name.

Of course, we add or substitute extemporaneous prayer, as appropriate, to address the specific need or thanksgiving the person is bringing forward.

This ministry was initiated by clergy. It is now offered by lay people with full clergy support and partnership.

A Healing Program
Changes Church
and Community

THE VERY REVEREND PETER ELLIOTT *is Dean of New Westminster and rector of Vancouver's Christ Church Anglican Cathedral.*

∾∾∾

How did the congregation react to the introduction of a healing ministry at the Sunday liturgy?

There was a lot of teaching in sermons and articles before we took this step. Each Sunday in Lent, one of the members of the healing team would speak for two minutes — two minutes only — about why the ministry of healing was important to them and what actually happened when people went over to the healing station to be prayed for. During Lent three congregational workshops were offered on the meaning of healing, sharing personal experiences of healing, and looking at the ways of our model healer, the Lord Jesus.

At first, some members of the congregation thought it was too public. Everybody would know that a person was in trouble if that person were seen at the healing station. One parishioner recalled growing up in a low-church Anglican parish where the Holy Communion was celebrated only four times a year, and many people would leave before communion was administered. People then drew the conclusion that anyone who received communion must be in trouble — an exact parallel to the objections being raised about the public nature of the healing ministry.

The healing team explained that some people came to offer thanksgiving for something good that had happened in their lives. They explained that in the course of our lives we all have times when we need healing. Furthermore, if the congregation saw a person being prayed for, they might also be concerned for that person and offer prayer. Sometimes one of the clergy would go to the healing team for prayers. Gradually the objections died away, and people accepted that everybody has difficult moments and can be helped by the healing ministry. In fact, some people have been attracted to the cathedral because of it. The word has got out.

After receiving comments from the congregation, we decided to make healing prayer a constant feature of the Sunday eucharist, beginning in October 1995.

When people ask for healing prayers, are they asking for cures for sickness or for help in dealing with other difficulties in their lives?

Some ask for help in physical sickness, but we make a clear distinction between curing and healing. Healing covers emotional and spiritual affliction as well as physical affliction.

Cancer is all around in modern society. People add prayer to the other treatments they are receiving, and while a cure is not always possible, many say that the prayer has helped them to deal with the disease, with all its physical and mental and emotional anguish.

Many people request prayers not for themselves, but for other people in need. I remember a couple who showed up regularly on Sundays. They came from Ottawa and were in Vancouver because the man's mother was dying. All during her illness, the funeral, and the closing down of his mother's apartment, they attended the cathedral and found support in the healing prayers.

How is the healing team set up and trained?

The team has grown from about five members originally to about twenty now. They make an intentional decision about whether to grow in number or not, and if they decide that an increase is necessary, they consider which members of the congregation it might be appropriate to ask. When a new person agrees to become involved, the person who invited them becomes their mentor, explaining the ministry and how it works. Then the new person has an appointment with me at which we discuss the importance of the ministry. Finally the person is commissioned during Sunday worship.

The team meets a few times a year to do business — establishing rotas, discussing concerns, finding out how people are feeling about their healing work, and evaluating the ministry. In addition, twice a year the team meets for a day-long session of training when a resource person may make a presentation. Our next meeting will focus on contemplative prayer, because people involved in the healing ministry often feel depleted and recognize the necessity of attending to their own spiritual growth and their own connection with God.

What other pastoral programs in the parish support the healing ministry?

If anyone has a particular need or knows someone who has, they call in their name to the office and the name is put on a list, which is circulated weekly among the Prayer Link members, about thirty at present.

We also have a program called Pastoral Care Resource Persons. These are lay people who are trained to provide pastoral care for people in the congregation. They take an eight-week course, meeting weekly, and when they have completed the requirements, they are assigned to pastor one or two or three people.

Of course, not everyone in the congregation needs constant pastoral care. Most are in a stable situation, although they may occasionally have particular problems to deal with. An ongoing program of small group ministries — study groups, for example — provides ways to meet and stay in touch with people in a large downtown church like ours. We are convinced that helping people to feel a sense of community is part of healing.

But there are always people in crisis or dealing with chronic illness. These are the people we assign to the pastoral care resource persons. The resource persons visit in homes and hospitals and take the sacrament to those who cannot get to church.

An associated group is the Cathedral Centre for Spiritual Direction, which includes two spiritual directors, one full time and one half time, who offer in-depth spiritual direction and other kinds of counselling to those who want it. Both of the spiritual directors are also certified clinical counsellors. And one of the initial questions they have to answer is whether a person really needs counselling or spiritual direction. The line between the two is often fuzzy.

The Centre for Spiritual Direction is more or less self-supporting through client fees, and we're raising a little bit of money for a foundation that will cover the expense for people who can't afford to pay for the services. Of the two spiritual directors, both lay women, one has a master's degree in spiritual direction from General Seminary in New York, and the other is certified as a spiritual director but also works as a Jungian analyst.

What theological and spiritual understatings underlie the healing ministry?

When you look at the ministry of Jesus as described in the Bible and count the ways in which he was involved with people, you see him as friend and you see him as teacher. But throughout the gospels, it is especially clear that Jesus was involved in the healing of people — body, mind, and spirit. Also, the record of the early church in the Acts of the Apostles and in the Epistles of Saint Paul places a strong emphasis on the role of the Christian community in the healing of individuals.

We take seriously Jesus' words that he has come to give life and give it abundantly, but sometimes life comes too abundantly for people and gives them more than they can deal with. By prayer, a person's life experience is put into a broader perspective — a perspective of eternity, a perspective of the divine. In a very intimate and personal moment, those two worlds intermingle: the divine desire for human well-being and health, and the human being's experience of disintegration or difficulty. Bringing the disintegration and difficulty into the context of church and the sacred liturgy, and also into the intimacy of a personal encounter, changes people.

When people come forward for healing, bringing a particular problem and talking about it as we pray for them, they can experience an emotional release, which often includes tears. They relax with a sense of relief, knowing that they have brought their problem to the deepest or highest spiritual resource possible.

A couple of Sundays ago, I looked over to the healing station from where I was administering communion and saw a member of the congregation, a man in his fifties, whom I knew had just lost his job. He was a businessman who, three years ago, might have said that it was embarrassing to have a healing station in public view. But there he was, simply taking his problem — a very significant one for a middle-aged man — offering it to God, and receiving the ministry of the church.

How has the healing ministry affected the church's role in the community at large?

The healing ministry builds community in a kind of wonderful way and increases people's sense that the church has something very directly to do with the circumstances of a person's life. People of all ages make use of it. I've seen children present themselves for healing. It's one of the ways they learn about what the church does and how Jesus Christ is alive in the proclamation of the church. In its downtown location, the cathedral attracts not only its own regular congregation, but also business people who work in the area, shoppers, tourists, and street people. Some of them come because they have heard about the healing ministry, and especially on Thursdays people come from other parishes.

I come from a liberal catholic background. I was, frankly, somewhat suspicious of the ministry of healing before my experience at the cathedral. I worried that it might be manipulative or not quite genuine. Since coming to the cathedral and seeing the great care, the gentleness, the intimacy, and the confidentiality that surrounds the ministry of healing, I've been convinced of its importance and its power. And I've experienced it myself, both as a person who prays for people and as a person who has been prayed for any number of times.

THE WOUNDED HEALER RECEIVES HEALING

SHIRLEY HARDING *has been a member of the heal-ing team at Christ Church Cathedral for many years. When diagnosed with breast cancer, she found herself in need of the ministrations the team provides.*

Can you describe something of your experience of spiritual healing?

My experience of spiritual healing is very deep and en-compasses many different aspects, including laying on of hands, a First Nations yiwipi ceremony, prayers of so many friends, family, communities, and those I really didn't know, and the hugs and support of those who were closely involved with my healing. Let's be very clear: spiritual healing is God's alone, and we offer ourselves to the Spirit/God/Creator for heal-ing, never knowing God's will for us. In the prayerful healing I received, I found a deep peace that allowed me to go on knowing I was being cradled and held by a loving God.

In 1992, I was given a diagnosis of metastatic bilateral breast cancer with words like "advanced, infiltrating" delivered in a very cold clinical fashion. Needless to say, I was in great shock, full of fear and confusion, and yet never without hope.

My family and friends began immediately to pray. They organized a powerful meditation circle which reached across this country into the USA and farther. Every day at 6:30 a.m. my husband and I received the prayers and hope that came from all those people meditating at the same time for my healing. With that came a peace that took away my fear and the knot deep in my gut.

At the same time I had just begun to work for the National Anglican Church in a position whose mandate was healing and reconciliation with First Nations who had suffered from the Anglican-run residential schools. Healing was the focus, as determined by the First Nations themselves. Was it a coincidence that I was the person searching desperately for my own healing and at the same time offering myself as a healing presence for the church?

I attended a healing gathering sponsored by the Niaka'pamux Nation in the summer of 1992, and this began a journey of preparation for a sacred healing ceremony. When I was offered a yiwipi ceremony for my healing I was completely overcome with humility and gratitude. These same people who were engaged in a healing process because of the Anglican residential school in their territory were reaching out to me, a white person, who represented the church that had damaged them. I will never forget that.

I began three intense months of prayer and preparation for the ceremony. One of the great things I learned during this time was to pray for myself. Praying for myself was something I had not been taught by my church. Praying for my healing many times a day at the river became my daily routine, and forever changed my practice of prayer. The ceremony itself was very powerful and rooted in very ancient beliefs. I felt very cared for.

At the same time I regularly attended the Thursday healing service at Christ Church Cathedral and received the laying on of hands and prayers for healing. It was only there that I was able to cry and let go of my fear. I was supported in every way by the cathedral parish, with love, friendship, and through the prayer list. I received spiritual healing from hugs, the look of compassion in the eyes of people, cards with words of encouragement, and so much more.

A friend whom I had supported through the same experience the year before came to Vancouver to be with me. That was a great gift because I really needed someone who had survived to be a witness to "life after breast cancer."

Spiritual healing wears many faces, and always the face of love and compassion that only a Great and Holy Spirit can give.

How has your experience of healing affected your work as a member of the cathedral's healing team?

After the many blessings I had received from the cathedral and because it had been my community since 1970, I wanted to give something back for all that I had received. By 1993 I was ready to be involved with the healing ministry team again, having been part of it in the 1970s. The healing ministry remains a very important part of my life and my commitments. It is a great privilege to be part of it.

As part of our education we began reading scientific material from doctors who supported what we always believed about the power of prayer in the healing process. When Dr. Larry Dossey spoke at a public lecture at the cathedral, we felt very thankful, energized, and affirmed in the ministry we were about.

I also offer myself to any who have just received a diagnosis of breast cancer, because it is so important to see and hear from someone who has survived. I have accepted the treatments the medical profession had to offer me. I am a former nurse who knew only the "medical way," and so my journey of discovery through other means of healing has been life giving. I believe very much in supporting your own immune system through any of the means available to us. What I have learned is always passed on to others for them to at least think about. Empowering myself in my own healing process gives me hope. I continue to see a naturopath every month, who monitors my wellness and treats me accordingly, as well as going for my check-up at the cancer clinic every six months.

One of the other groups at the cathedral is the One-One Cancer Support. It works as a one-to-one support for someone who has been diagnosed with cancer. The appropriate person in the parish who has had the same cancer and treatment is paired up with the one in need.

My own healing transformed my prayer life into one of thankfulness — thankfulness for my healing, for every new day and all that life offers us. I also learned this from the prayers of First Nations people. Thanksgiving is always at the heart of all their prayers.

Henri Nouwen in his book *The Wounded Healer* describes the wounded healer as someone who must look after his own wounds at the same time as being prepared to offer healing to the wounds of others. I have been blessed with being able to know the power of God's healing at the darkest and most vulnerable time of my life. Now I am able to offer myself to others from my deepest, most wounded, and healed place.